4th Edition

audio
MADE EASY
(Or How To Be A Sound Engineer Without Really Trying)

By Ira White

HAL•LEONARD®

ISBN-13: 978-1-4234-2014-9
ISBN-10: 1-4234-2014-4

Published by:
Hal Leonard Corporation
7777 W. Bluemound Road
P.O. Box 13819
Milwaukee, WI 53213

 Library of Congress Cataloging-in-Publication Data

White, Ira.
 Audio made easy / by Ira White. -- 4th ed.
    p. cm.
 ISBN-13: 978-1-4234-2014-9
 1. Sound--Recording and reproducing 2. Sound--Equipment and supplies. I. Title.
 TK7881.4W484 2007
 621.389'3--dc22

                              2006031217

Printed in the U.S.A.

Fourth Edition

7777 W. BLUEMOUND RD. P.O. BOX 13819 MILWAUKEE, WI 53213

Visit Hal Leonard online at **www.halleonard.com**

CONTENTS

CD TRACKS

1. INTRODUCTION

THIS IS YOUR BRAIN...THIS IS AUDIO...THIS IS YOUR BRAIN ON AUDIO

As far back as I can remember, people have been asking for a complete book on professional audio that they can understand. Unfortunately, most books only cover certain aspects of audio, and are wrought with pages of formulas and abstract elements that tax the interest of the average person in a world where most would believe transient response is what you get when you ask a bum a question. Or that Hertz is just a car rental company. Not exactly.

A lot of people want to get involved in sound or recording for the fun and fulfillment of it. They're not interested in writing a thesis for their doctorate. They're probably not going to be asked to design and run a system for Shania Twain. However, they *would* like useful information, a sense of accomplishment, and some aural excitement without too much pain (Hertz?). Beyond that, audio interests can be pursued as far as the heart desires.

So I decided to write this book covering a little of everything without becoming too tedious. It's based on my experiences and the many questions asked of me by colleagues and customers, and it delves a little deeper into some of the more misunderstood areas such as digital mixers, using EQ, speaker specifics, and recording techniques. In it, I wish to furnish real world solutions and tips that will show results and not just raise more questions. I wish to accommodate a variety of equipment budgets and provide a firm foundation on which to build audio wisdom. I wish to give you the capability to soar to new heights, and achieve any lofty dream you may hold dear! I wish to retire at age fifty with lots of money!!

Well, maybe I'm getting ahead of myself, but at least we can accomplish something along the way. I'm game if you are.

Ira White

P.S. You'll notice some numerical indicators next to certain audio terms. These are listed in the index at the back of the book, and refer you to additional related sections on the topic being discussed.

Also, even if you're only interested in a particular aspect of audio, I encourage you to read this whole book. There are tips and information within every section and application that should be helpful to you. Besides, it isn't that long. In the time it takes to add a room addition to your house or take an Italian vacation, you could have read this book and still had time for a shower. (Assuming you're a slow reader.)

This is a work of nonfiction. The characters, incidents, and dialogues are products of the author's imagination but are not to be construed as unreal. Any resemblance to actual events or persons, living or dead, is entirely intentional though probably grossly exaggerated.

2. SOUND PSYCHE

THE PRIDE AND THE PASSION

Music is an art, and engineering is just an extension of that art. You should first understand that you are an integral part of the overall product — not just a button pusher, but an artist that makes spontaneous decisions based on what you hear. The song is the subject, the instruments are the paint, the tone and balance are the brush strokes, and the room (or recorder) is the canvas. Your equipment ultimately gives you the capability to create the overall picture, to skillfully mix the colors, to move yourself and others to an emotional response. And like any passionate endeavor, the fact that you are working hard and starving at the same time is mostly hidden by the enjoyment of your quest.

The only problem is that you need to master the basics well enough for them to run on automatic while you dedicate your time to creating. Like riding a bike you can concentrate on where you're going and not on how to turn the pedals. And you need to feel comfortable and confident in your capabilities, especially in one-shot live situations. Just as in scuba diving, if you panic you drown. Don't be intimidated and keep a cool head. Things are rarely as bad as they seem, and you'll find that peace of mind promotes good judgement and will rub off on others around you creating a sense of security and trust. That's a positive influence on the most volatile variable of working with others — chemistry.

> *Like riding a bike, you can concentrate on where you're going and not on how to turn the pedals.*

THE GOLDEN RULE

. . . and speaking of chemistry, I'd like to mention something about social interaction. When working with other people, the fun can quickly depart if we eccentric artists get into adversarial relationships. We often try to push our opinions on others which only puts them on the defensive. We all need to work together, but I still need to know that I'm in control of my responsibilities.

The way I do this is to always try to show concern for another's views. Sometimes they're right. Sometimes just politely explaining when they're not, in overly technical jargon that neither of us can understand, helps. In either case, I'll generally make a point of periodically (and sincerely) asking how things sound to those concerned. Once their defenses are down and they feel secure in having received sufficient consideration, I can maintain reasonable control in peace. Mutual respect develops. Everybody wins. In those exceptions where it doesn't work, blackmail is a nice backup plan.

THE BROKEN RULE

I'll be passing on ideas in this book that will establish constructive guidelines. The ironic thing is that once you've mastered them, it's time to throw many of them out. Rules can't teach you how to create, but only how someone else created. It's up to you to blaze new paths. Once you've got a little knowledge tucked away, you'll find that common sense goes a long way towards experimentation and discovery. And once you've beaten every new idea to death, you'll invariably learn that less is more.

I never fully realized how this had applied to my engineering development until I tried learning about stage lighting. I read about focal lengths, lumens, ellipsoidals and fresnels, Roscolux colors … I was so proud of my wealth of knowledge. And then I saw an Emmy-award-winning lighting guy do almost everything with a few par cans and four basic colors. I should have asked him how he did it without the other junk, but he probably would have said, "Sounds like you've been reading a book."

So don't let rules hold you back. And don't overcomplicate things. Keep it simple, keep an open mind, and don't hesitate to ask questions. You can learn something from everybody, and each little tidbit can be filed away in your cerebral library of audio wisdom to be called upon in crucial decisions when you least expect it. As soon as you stop testing the limits, you will go no further. Have fun, be young, drink Pepto Bismol.

3. THE SOURCE BE WITH YOU

If you want specs, get a spec sheet. If you want detailed features and operation, get an owner's manual. But if you want excellent general info and brilliant tips. . . welcome to the club! Hopefully, we'll take the mysticism out of audio equipment and learn how to use this stuff, taking each in its proper order of signal flow. We begin where it all starts — at the source.

ON THE LEVEL

There is a great variety of sound-producing instruments which you will most likely be dealing with in your audio aspirations, many of which are already electronic in nature. These include CD players, tape decks, stereo or instrument preamplifiers, keyboards and sound modules, etc. These can plug straight into appropriate audio equipment and transfer their sounds directly and accurately. Acoustical sounds such as vocals and acoustic instruments cannot. They must first be converted to electronic signals to be used, so we add an incredible variety of microphones to our list of sources to accomplish this task. Using which-ones-where will be discussed shortly.

Our first concern is levels. Though all these products lack the higher voltage to drive speakers (amplifiers do that), they nevertheless have a low-level voltage that we can express in a unit of measure called the **decibel** (or **dB**) that will let us know how potentially loud each can be in relation to the other. Their dB output rating, or *gain*[1], will be important when integrating with other equipment and can be classed in two general categories — **mic level** and **line level**.

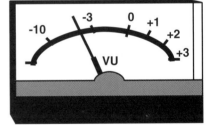

Mic-level sources are the lowest, and generally associated with *passive* sources (those not driven by electrical or battery power). Microphones themselves are typically in the -60dB to -50dB range, electric guitars around -30 to -20dB. *Active* (powered) line-level sources like keyboards and mixers are above -20dB, and can get up to +4dB average peak (*unity gain*[2]) or even higher outputs. If you ever checked the meter on a cassette deck with a tape playing, you saw that the meter read from around -20dB to +4dB (a 24dB range), and there was a big difference between the loudest and softest stuff. Now imagine adding another -40dB to the bottom range for a total of at least 64dB between our lowest and highest sources, and you can get some idea of the great variations in equipment levels. But be not dismayed for, wonder of wonders, the mixer we use will allow us to accommodate for these differences.

MICROPHONES

Mic choices can be one of the hardest decisions because most people don't get the chance to compare many out in the real world. There are usually three or more nice choices in the same class, though one will most likely have the nicest sound or price or both to set it apart from the rest. Knowing which one takes a little bit of research. As with most products, the more you spend, the more likely you'll get higher quality. But these days, there are some top-notch mics in almost every price range, so don't let budget kill your expectations.

When shopping for mics such as vocal handhelds, compare through accurate speakers (preferably studio monitors) or try to get them on a trial-and-return basis to make sure they live up to your real-world needs. Test the mic from about 3 inches. Listen for a smooth and musical sound. One mistake novices make is to gravitate to a mic that has the most treble and bass in its response. This can indicate undesirable peaks or a lack of mids. The ideal should be a natural, balanced sound as the starting point. Then you will have all the necessary sonic components to manipulate as your heart, ears, and audio system demand. Also check handling noise by tapping the casings, and off-axis rejection by talking into the side of the mic which indicates how well it rejects feedback. Finally, check industry reviews in various pro audio magazines. (I discovered some of the best-kept secrets there.) All in all, you'll discover significant differences between models. Now, let's cover some information on microphone types.

A **dynamic** mic is a little speaker in reverse. Sound waves in the air vibrate the mic diaphragm, moving a tiny coil back and forth around a magnet and generating a low voltage signal. Dynamics are durable, economical, and usually have good response within close distances. Though they have limited sensitivity for picking up distant sources, this can be a plus in live sound where isolation is critical. This means the mic doesn't pick up things you don't want it to. Styles include *ball mics* with a built-in windscreen to minimize breath pop from vocals, and *pencil mics* which are designed more as instrumental mics since they don't have the windscreen. Good affordable dynamics are around $100 to $300. Some popular standards include the Shure SM and Beta series and the Audix OM series.

A **condenser** mic is designed with a more sensitive diaphragm for increased frequency response and distance pickup. Unlike a dynamic mic, it generates signal through a change in capacitance between two charged elements, and requires a voltage source to drive circuits in the mic or an associated electronics pack. (Don't worry, I'm not sure *I* understood what I just said.) The voltage needs to be supplied by an integral battery or an external source called ***phantom power***[3] which is available on most professional mixers. (No, it's not a power boost for your system!) Condenser styles include a variety of *pencil* (end-address) and *side-address* models, the latter being the heftier studio models with a large diaphragm that picks up from the side. Economical cardioid condensers like the Audix ADX51, Rode NT1A, Audio-Technica AT4040, or AKG C451 can range from $200 to $600, while various switchable pattern and tube circuit models typically run from $500 up depending on how much you want to impress your "clients."

(Again, check industry reviews for current "hot picks.") Less-expensive battery-operated condensers can be had for under $150 and will pass in budget situations, but lack the quality and level handling of the phantom-powered models. There are also special miniature condensers designed for choirs, podiums, instruments, and other live applications.

Condensers are essential for studio recording, acoustic instrument pickup, and distance pickup, but less so for live handheld vocals. The handhelds cost more than dynamics, and their components are a bit more fragile. Personally, I find handheld condensers lacking the isolation and feedback rejection of current quality dynamics like the Audix OM5 and OM6, and I prefer to avoid potential noise problems that can occur with 48 volts of phantom power going through a stressed mic cable.

A lesser-known design is the **ribbon** mic, currently offered by just a few manufacturers such as Royer and Beyer. It gets its name from the very small, thin metal ribbon that serves as its element. Though sensitive like a condenser, most are passive (non-powered) like a dynamic and have a low output level. Besides being expensive, its delicate ribbon is easily prone to damage. You won't see these very often and they aren't essential in any particular application, though many have a unique "warm and sweet" sound.

EXPLORING THE POLES

Mics are available in a variety of pickup, or polar, patterns. **Omnidirectional** mics pick up sound in all directions, making them unsuitable in most live applications where directed pickup and *feedback*[4] rejection are crucial. Consequently, **unidirectional** mics (which includes ball mics) are designed with special vents allowing sounds from the rear and sides to enter the capsule and be cancelled. Be aware that if you try to look "cool" by wrapping your hand around the head of a ball mic, you cover up its vents and turn it into an omnidirectional that's prone to feedback and bad sound! Another unidirectional trait is **proximity effect**. If a source such as vocal is within 6 inches of a unidirectional mic, bass frequencies become disproportionately stronger. Some mics have a bass rolloff switch to compensate for this, or it can be controlled at the mixer by turning down the low EQ if the sound is boomy or muddy.

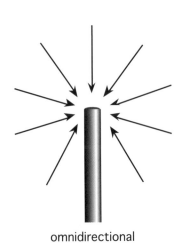

omnidirectional

unidirectional

Cardioid design unidirectionals have a medium pickup pattern, say 100°, around the front of the mic and the most rejection of sound at the rear. **Hypercardioids** are usually more expensive and have a tighter pattern of maybe 70°, making them less prone to feedback with maximum rejection to either side of the rear. (One of the most affordable is the Audix OM3.)

Supercardioid is tighter still and designed more for narrow distance pickup, many times in the form of long "shotgun" condenser mics. **Bidirectional** is a lesser-used studio pattern that picks up from both front and rear with greatest rejection on either side. It is only available in special-design dynamics and in studio condensers with switchable patterns.

MIC TECHNIQUES

Since many of you will likely be in a less-than-ideal room environment, I choose to focus on close-micing techniques good for studio and live applications. With a good studio condenser, any instrument will sound natural when picked up from 3 feet or more, but you'll also pick up bad room acoustics, noises, and any other nearby instruments with the extra level required. Close micing sounds more "in-your-face" and is definitely necessary when isolation is important, but mic placement is critical. This is because it takes a little bit of distance for tones from different parts of an instrument to finally mix to become its complete sound. The bigger the instrument, the greater the distance. The trick in close micing is to pick up a part of the instrument that best represents the whole thing. Subtle or subjective corrections may be accomplished through mic choice or mixer EQ.

If you choose to *stereo mic*[5] distant sources for recording, you can use a simple "V" configuration. Place the heads or bases of the mics together (not touching) to form an angle of 75°–90°, each one aiming toward opposite sides of your source area. I slightly prefer the bases together because the separated elements offer a little more stereo imaging while simulating the distance between our ears with air in between, a typical characteristic of sound engineers.

Now we get to the part where common sense goes a long way. *Where should the mic be placed?* Where the instrument sounds the best. *Where does the instrument sound the best?* Listen to it, Sherlock.

Acoustic Guitar: Let's start with a guy playing acoustic guitar. First, listen to the guitar from about 3–5 feet away. This natural sound will be your reference. (If it sounds like garbage, put the mic anywhere and revert to prayer.) We'll be placing the mic 6–12 inches away from the front so the picking hand won't hit it. Now pretend your ear is the mic, and listen around all the spots within 12 inches in front of the guitar. If it sounds too dull, don't put the mic there. If it sounds too thin or hollow, ditto. If it sounds about right, put the mic there and you're ready to roll. My usual spot is just to the side of the sound hole at the end of the fret board in front of the high-end strings. For close stereo micing, I'll prefer another somewhere around the bridge of the guitar.

First rule: *trust your ears.* (You didn't know you had all the answers stuck on the side of your head, did you?) Choose a spot with the sound closest to what you're looking for. The only drawback is if you have no clue as to what you want to hear. Solution: start listening to a lot of good music and develop preferences. *Your* sound is probably written in your DNA and you just need to draw it out.

For acoustic guitar, a good condenser is preferred for stage or studio. Built-in pickups can be more convenient for live use, but most don't emulate the natural sound for critical recording in the studio. However, it can be helpful to record mic and pickup combinations to take advantage of both — the natural sound of micing and the unique tone and isolation of the pickup. If you're feeding an acoustic pickup direct through long lines such as a snake (an extension cable of multiple mic lines), use a ***direct box***[6]. I've also used a good wireless lapel mic in live situations with some excellent results. Clip it on the sound hole in such a way that it's not setting in the hole and EQ as needed.

Electric Guitar: With electric guitar cabinets, you have the same situation as with an acoustic instrument. Different tones come from the center and sides of the speaker cone, any ports or openings, and the cabinet itself. Listen close to areas of the speaker and you'll notice that the sound isn't the same 5 feet away. A particular problem I've found is that many guitarists have their cabinets on the floor with the higher frequencies shooting under them in a narrow pattern. They adjust their tone for the very "warm" sound they're hearing while high-end "bite" is actually cranking out at speaker level. This is why many guitar rigs sound so thin and edgy from the mic and audience perspective. Better that the speaker is raised or angled up so the guitarist can hear and adjust his tone more accurately.

It's up to you to decide whether you want the close or distant sound or a combination of both, and mic accordingly. I usually mic within 6 inches at the side of the cone pointing toward the center, and control the "edgy" treble by cutting back on the mixer high EQ. This brings out more of the guitar warmth. Another mic can be placed back 5 feet or more in the studio for natural ambience if desired. My favorite mics going up the price scale: Shure SM57, Audix OM3, Beyer M69, Sennheiser 421, or a *large-diaphragm* studio condenser.

Though I prefer to mic, electric guitar can also be run direct to the mixer when using a guitar preamp, pedal, or "pod" designed for this purpose. The problem with direct guitar is that optimum tone can often be dependent on the sound being processed and punched through a classic guitar cabinet, particularly when it comes to distortion. Experiment. Direct or otherwise, you may find the unique sound that makes for an international star . . . or draws complaints from the neighbors next door.

Bass Guitar: I almost always favor running electric bass direct. There are rarely unforgiving effects to deal with, and you get accurate and isolated pickup of the instrument. Once in a great while in the studio, there comes along a bass rig that sounds so fantastic that it would be a sin not to let the rest of the world share in the experience. In those cases, I will most likely use one of my Audix kick drum mics or a large-diaphragm condenser and record it with the direct signal for added flexibility. If it's a good bass, this should be one of the easier instruments to capture well.

Drums: This is the toughest single undertaking for most engineers and requires the most resources. And because drums collectively cover the broadest frequency range of any instrument, it shares a place with vocals as one of the most crucial parts of your mix, studio or live. I suggest a minimum of six mics and a compatible mixer with at least three bands of *EQ*[7], two sweepable, on each channel. (If you're already intimidated, it may be time to run out and buy an electronic set or a drum machine. You won't be the first, and I actually like some of the upscale electronic drums these days for live sound, especially in smaller rooms where acoustic drum levels can be an overwhelming problem.) If it's a less demanding application or you're a jazz purist, you're off the hook. Set up a stereo pair of good condensers over or just in front of the set and you'll get that natural sound. Add an optional mic on the kick drum to control and accentuate it as well.

Individual drums require close micing to isolate them from each other and give us more control of the mix. Placement is best just over the edge of the top head within an inch or two. When desired tone can't be achieved with the proper mic, placement, or drum tuning, it can be assisted by the mixer EQ. I'll offer some notes based on my drum micing experience and EQ techniques, which are discussed further in the Mixer chapter if you get confused. After becoming more familiar with EQ itself, you may then wish to refer back to these notes. Or you may regard them as useless suggestions for what you're attempting to achieve. Your choice.

Many engineers use *noise gates*[8] on mics to isolate drums, and sometimes they may be necessary. I prefer not to use them for several reasons. Most isolation problems can be controlled by mic choice, placement, and EQ. Also, some bleed from other mics can give the drums more of a live sound when balanced effectively. So don't feel it necessary to run and buy out the noise gate stock at your local music store. Better to use the money for better mics. (If you have a digital mixer, you'll likely have free built-in gates to experiment with.)

In live sound, clear drum shields help significantly in reducing drum levels into the house, and give the sound engineer more control over the drum sound. Use shields at least 5 feet high and, if there are hard walls behind the drums, either provide acoustical wall treatment or use a couple of free-standing sound absorbing baffles in a V-shape behind the drums to deter reflections.

Kick Drum: This requires a specialized mic like an Audix D4 or AKG D112 to handle the excessive air pressure and low frequencies. It should be placed inside the shell within 6 inches of and aimed towards the beater head to maximize high-frequency attack. Low-end without high-end punch is just a dull chest-pumping thud (but then a few people like that). Some potential problem areas: excessive bass below 100Hz, muddiness in the 100–300Hz range, and/or a need for more attack around 2–4kHz.

Snare: Any of the mics listed for electric guitar (except the large studio condenser) or drum-specific models are appropriate for snare. A major problem here is bleed from the high hat, especially if the drummer is crazy enough to use Rude cymbals! I minimize this by pointing it away from the hat just over the edge of the snare under the first tom and using a hypercardioid mic if necessary. Placing the head of the mic at the edge allows it to pick up more of the snares underneath. Placing it in over the snare head will usually result in more of a dull pop, often forcing you to boost high end and increase hat bleed. Problems may be a dull or hollow bump in the 300–600Hz range or a need for more high end from 2–6kHz. In the studio, you could mic the bottom head as well to control snare balance if you have the resources.

Hi Hat: Mic this with a condenser pointing straight down a few inches above the outside edge opposite the drummer. Isolation is generally not a problem, but I prefer to roll out all frequencies below 1kHz to eliminate noise and isolate the hat, and boost above 12kHz if needed for a sweet high end.

Toms: Mic just over the outside edge pointing across the head with the same type mics used for snare. You may need to roll out some dullness in the 200–400Hz range and add high end at 2–5kHz. (If I'm experiencing some bleed from large cymbals, I'll prefer closer to 5kHz to avoid mid range harshness.) If you have to pick up two toms with one mic, pick the smallest toms and use a cardioid mic with good low end. For this or a fat sound on floor tom, I'll often use a tight kick drum mic like an ATM25 or Audix D4 to accentuate those lower frequencies.

Overheads: Use a good condenser in the middle of the set about a foot above the highest cymbal. If two mics are available, use a stereo pair angled out toward opposite groups of cymbals. I roll out everything below 200Hz to keep the low end tight on the rest of the set. Frequencies up to 800Hz may also be reduced to maximize cymbal pickup and minimize ambient pickup of the set. In smaller live venues, you can often eliminate overheads since the cymbals will carry and may get picked up by vocal mics anyway (absent a drum shield, of course).

Percussion: Use overhead-style micing for this. Dynamic mics will do fine for stronger instruments like congas, bongos, and cowbells. Live setups can also be picked up with a good lapel mic, wired or wireless, on the percussionist himself allowing freedom of movement with the various instruments. From the chest location, point the lapel element downward instead of upward if it's a unidirectional.

(Note: If you use electronic drums, I recommend splitting off at least kick, snare, hi hat, and the rest of the set through four different outputs to the mixer so the engineer has independent control of these like an acoustic set. I can handle the "rest of the set" through one channel since high and low EQ can control balance between cymbals and toms. Many electronic sets have this output capability, and I would make it a priority in a purchase.)

Acoustic Piano: Trust your ears and listen around the instrument soundboard for the sweet spots. A safe and accurate bet in solo grand piano recording is a stereo pair of condenser mics placed 3–5 feet away with the piano lid fully open. Of course, with the distance, room acoustics are going to be a significant aspect of the sound. If you don't have access to a good room or if you simply need more isolation, you can mic inside about a foot high and angled towards each side of the soundboard for even pickup. If the mics are too low, strings closest to the elements will peak on you. If you desire a brighter sound with more attack, move mics closer to the hammers. (For isolation in a group performance, position loud instruments like drums and brass farther away from the piano.)

In live sound, I've found it possible to get a reasonably balanced sound and good isolation from a single unidirectional condenser if the grand is a 7–9 footer. With the lid at the lowest open position, place the mic on a boom over the strings about halfway in from the side. The mic should be pointing to the back end, parallel to the soundboard with the rear of the mic near the hammers. Height should be close to the lid without touching it. The reason this works is that the mic is directed to the back to maximize bass and warmth, while the normally peaky mids and highs are off axis and rejected for a smoothing and balancing effect. It's not as effective with a smaller grand which lacks some warmth and bass to balance with the higher strings. Some EQ may still be necessary to compensate for low mid resonance off the soundboard and lid. This is usually cut somewhere between 250Hz and 400Hz. Some high-end dynamics or flat condenser *boundary* mics like the Crown PCC-160 do okay, but I avoid using omnidirectional PZM mics.

When it comes to spinet uprights, I've never gotten an acceptable sound micing from the top, and trying to mic from the front usually picks up too much pedal noise. So I find it more convenient to mic from the rear. Usually the second opening in the frame from the bass side gives me a decent sound with a single mic pointing right into the rear soundboard. For stereo, just find a good spot towards the other side. Frankly, spinets tend to sound pretty unimpressive, so I'd opt for a good electronic keyboard if a grand isn't available.

Orchestra: To capture that natural quality I keep referring to, orchestral or band instruments should be mic'ed from at least 1' and ensembles or sections at least 3 feet away. The distance also minimizes the "edginess" of strings and the mechanical noises of some instruments. In performances, isolation doesn't take priority over proper mic placement, and some ambience or bleed can actually add dimension. The greater concern is to keep louder instruments such as percussion and brass away from the softer and lesser-projecting instruments like piano and strings.

In recording, you could just stereo mic the room to capture a performance as the audience hears it and eliminate mixing altogether. But even when using a stereo pair in a good concert hall, close micing would allow for subtle and individual control of sections where needed. For live solo instruments in bands or ensembles, there are also a number of small clip-on mic designs available for wired and wireless applications.

Strings: Like acoustic guitar, stringed instruments are relatively low in level and require the most consideration in pickup and isolation, so always use a good condenser. For a single violin, viola, cello or string bass, point the mic towards the bridge and *f*-hole area. For ensembles, center the mic over the group and slightly angle it away from louder instrument sections if necessary. Treat harp like an acoustic guitar and mic individually from the side and slightly above the soundboard where it sounds balanced.

Reeds & Woodwinds: For isolating one or two instruments, you can mic near the end or bell. With ensembles, center in front of the group. Flutes, oboes, and bassoons will always be picked up from above. Good dynamic mics will do okay for small groups of two or three.

Brass: Dynamics will pass here, too, but a condenser will cover a larger section. Since horns are directional, be sure to get enough distance on sections for a good blend of the whole group. French horn can be mic'ed from above and behind. (So why do they stick their fist in the bell? I think they're stashing something in there.)

Percussion: Due to the extreme frequency ranges involved from timpani to bells and cymbals, always try to use condensers. I can usually cover the whole section with one or two distant mics, so I tend to concentrate placement on making sure I get a full sound on timpani since the high-end stuff usually cuts through.

Vocals: Most of the microphones made are designed with vocals in mind, so there's no shortage of choices here including hands-free headworn and the newer mini-earworn omnidirectionals. (We'll cover their significant details and differences in the wireless chapter "Unplugged.") Most of the time you needn't worry about mic technique or placement since the performer is going to eat the mic anyway. Just hook them up, pass out the barbecue sauce, and set 'em loose. The rest, God willing, will be done at the mixer. If, on the other hand, someone is holding the mic at their waist or waving it around in hand gestures as they speak (yes, I have had people do that), you will have to *teach* them some mic technique.

In the studio, you'll hopefully have more control. Definitely use a good condenser here and try to keep the performer at least 3 inches away by offering him a Big Mac ahead of time. Even better, use a nylon pop-screen set in front of the mic to maintain distance and minimize breath pops. If the mic has a low roll-off switch, use it to further reduce muddiness or pops.

Harmony: There are two ways to mic harmony parts. One, as you have probably already figured out, is to mic each singer giving you the most isolation and total control of the mix. In multitrack recording, this can be done all together or overdubbing one voice at a time to allow each singer to concentrate on their part alone. Another acceptable way is to use one cardioid mic for multiple singers (maximum three per mic). In live situations with a good vocal ensemble, this will allow them to control most of their blend naturally so they can't blame you for poor balance.

I often prefer a stereo pair setup in the studio because it gives me the natural dimensional imaging of everybody being in a unique position in the mix due to placement and room ambience. I can wrap up to ten singers in a semicircle around the two mics. The biggest problem is when singers just aren't proficient enough to perform their parts well together. Then it's back to one track at a time.

Choir: This is more of a problem due to the sheer number of people and the distance of the mics from them. Always use unidirectional condensers. With the availability of more economical miniature hanging choir mics, it isn't essential to buy the more expensive studio condensers for live use, and sometimes they can be a disadvantage with their high sensitivity more prone to feedback and picking up extraneous noises.

I space out one mic for every four or five people across, two or three rows deep. (More rows may require additional rear mics, or just stick all the bad singers in the back and don't worry about it.) Assuming you're about 6' tall, stand on the first row and stretch your arm up in front of you at a 45° angle. I want the mic head just beyond your fingertips with it pointing at the back row. This method gets the mic closer to the overall source, picks up the back rows on axis, and slightly rejects the closer front row which would otherwise tend to be louder.

For more conservative sound situations such as recording or when you're not competing with orchestra or band levels, you may be able to cut the number of mics in half or use a stereo pair and place at a greater distance for a natural blend. Micing options can include gooseneck podium mics on stands (which use the same elements as the miniature hanging mics) or, for picking up smaller ensembles upstage or on front steps, wireless handhelds on stands to avoid a tripping hazard from cables along the floor.

If you're having trouble getting choir over full band and/or orchestra, try wireless handhelds or "invisible" mini-earworns on eight to ten primary singers. Be careful to blend them in so they don't stand out as soloists. (Of course, you can always raise level for a solo.) Omni earworns are especially good here since they will pick up a little from adjacent singers for a more natural choir effect.

Podium: Condensers come in several designs for this purpose including goosenecks from 12–18 inches (preferred) and hemispherical boundary mics. One quick note: these small condensers are not designed with close pickup in mind, and may be overloaded by powerful voices within 6 inches. Unless you prefer the sound quality of a heavy metal band through a Radio Shack PA and the wind noise of a class-3 hurricane, consider substituting a quality handheld in situations where pastors or others prefer to dine on the podium mic.

I spent a lot of time on this section because it's where it all starts. If you screw up here, you'll never fully recover later on. Mic technique is a common sense art, and will make everything else easier if done right. A final point would be to use mics like a light. Do you need a floodlight to cover a wide area? Do you need a narrower spot beam to project a little farther into the darkness? Where would you point it to best illuminate things evenly from center to sides? Mics work the same in reverse:

omnidirectional = lightbulb

cardioid = floodlight

hypercardioid = medium spot

supercardioid = narrow spot.

See the light?

4. UNPLUGGED

THE WONDERFUL WORLD OF WIRELESS

Hop on down to the local PA store, pick out an economical wireless mic, hook it up to your sound system, and let the fun begin! Unfortunately with many budding technological tools, this concept can fall right in there with E.T.: The Extra-Terrestrial and fast food that's good for you. Nobody promised audio geeks a rose garden, but my initial experiences even fell short of compost!

My introduction to wireless systems was in music retail back in the eighties. We were subjected to primitive low-cost systems which, at that time, all performed horribly. I naturally assumed poor quality, annoying sounds, signals dropping out, and frequent breakdowns were unavoidable aspects of wireless. That's why I lost faith, at least until I eventually heard some good wireless systems in the $1500 range. Finally we were getting some performance though such cost was still prohibitive for many consumers who needed these convenient tools—especially churches and local theatre that required multiple systems. The good news is that prices on wireless systems have been coming down while quality has consistently gone up.

Nonetheless, we still had unexpected problems arise as we combined multiple units, used them in different environments, and integrated them in various systems. It seemed our troubles had only just started. So began my quest for truth based on research, trial and error, and numerous soul-stirring revelations usually preceded by incredible stupidity. This chapter is a by-product intended to help you get more out of wireless microphone use and bring you up to date on some features, price ranges, things to look for, and potential problems to avoid or overcome.

I also want you to be aware of features that I've found to be most practical and dependable in wireless production. Some companies have done a good job of addressing these needs in design and performance over the years, and I would only encourage other manufacturers to show the same common sense and attention to detail in their product development. Let me go down my personal dream list:

1. Though the standard receiver chassis need not be rackmount, all should be *rackmountable* and it is best to include a simple rack kit with the item. Rackmounting reduces abuse and possible damage to the unit and its connections, and offers security and convenient transport for multiple systems. The receivers should also be designed for easy and stable vertical stacking when not rackmounted. A metal chassis is preferred over plastic.

2. Antenna should be mounted on the *front* of the receiver, not on the top or rear, to accommodate rackmounting. It's hard to believe there are companies still making rackmount units with antenna on the rear where they can't be extended in a rack. They may inform you that optional front-mounting accessories or an **antenna distribution system** for four receivers is available for a few hundred dollars more. Thankfully, some manufacturers are providing a front-mount option on their rack kits. Since antennas can suffer damage, they should also be easy to replace without major surgery.

3. Receiver output should be variable *line* level for better signal-to-noise ratio, especially when patched through longer lines or snakes. Mic-level outputs are simply not necessary with the input flexibility of current mixers. Having both 1/4" phone and balanced XLR connections is always a plus, and a related ground lift switch is a welcome feature to eliminate **ground loop**[11] hums. Since a lot of economical receivers use AC adapters (wall-warts) for their power, I would prefer the option of a compatible and economical **power distribution** unit that will use one plug and supply power for at least eight systems. (Since such a unit could work for numerous brands, the manufacturers should get together on a standard plug and power rating to assure it.)

4. Since lapel mics possess the greatest failure potential due to cable stress at the belt-pack connection, they should be easy to repair or economical to replace, or both. I've found lapels for $25 that sounded as good as $100 models and held up better. One cost-effective design by Azden utilizes a right angle mini-phone plug (also compatible with current Sennheiser EW systems) to maintain a low profile less prone to stress against the body and eliminate the sharp "u-turn" of the dangling mic cable. An appropriate relief feature for straight plugs would be connections on the underside of the beltpack instead of the top. Or simply providing a metal belt clip that can be flipped upside down would work. (A lot of systems now offer this feature.) And wouldn't it be loverly if all the wireless manufacturers adopted a standard right-angle plug, and made all mics and packs interchangeable? Hint, hint...

5. Transmitters should be *easy* to switch on, and there should be continuous "active" indication as opposed to the instantaneous LED blink of many systems. There should also be some indication of battery strength or at least when the battery grows weak. (We're now seeing transmitter battery meters in UHF displays.) All transmitters should have *silent on/off,* not the annoying "thump" evident on many units. And an on/off cover or "locking" feature on beltpacks is nice for avoiding accidental shutoff in theatrical presentations.

A WIRELESS OVERVIEW

Take a microphone and hook it up to its own miniature radio station, and you have a wireless mic system. This is comprised of a battery-operated transmitter that the mic is connected to, and a receiver that passes the signal on to our mixer inputs. Just as radio stations must transmit on different frequency channels, you need a different channel wireless system for each mic to operate them simultaneously.

VHF, or **V**ery **H**igh **F**requency, wireless systems have used the 169MHz to 215MHz frequency range. Manufacturers generally offer about fifteen to twenty VHF channels, but for each two systems you use, other "spurious" frequencies are created by their combined signals. By the time you get to eight, the air is getting a bit cluttered with frequencies. Too many can cause interference from receivers getting confused as to who their partner is. (Sounds like Hollywood, doesn't it?) Nevertheless, I have used up to twelve carefully matched systems of the same brand without much problem.

UHF, or **U**ltra **H**igh **F**requency, systems in ranges from 600MHz through 900MHz offer much tighter reception allowing more to be used without interference problems between them. In fact, Broadway shows may use as many as thirty-two or more! (Shoot, the battery budget alone probably rivals what the government pays for a hammer.) Unlike VHF, most UHF have user-switchable tuning so you can change to another frequency if a problem arises with one. Good UHF systems have come down to the cost of a decent VHF, around $300, so it's hard to justify a VHF purchase anymore. I have yet to hear any UHF or VHF significantly below that price that I would feel comfortable with.

Non-diversity VHF systems use a single-antenna receiver to pick up the signal, and will realistically transmit up to 50 feet indoors. (There are no single-antenna UHF systems that I know of.) **Diversity** wireless, usually $50 to $100 extra in VHF models, are dual-circuit antenna systems that improve reception range up to 100 feet indoors by automatically switching to the other antenna circuit if one starts to drop out. There are a few cheaper, non-diversity **dipole** VHF systems out there with two antennas for slightly stronger reception, but this is a bit deceptive since they are both tied to only one circuit.

The farther away the transmitters and receivers are from each other, the weaker the signal gets. Problems arise from sheer distance or when original and reflected transmission signals arrive at an antenna simultaneously, canceling each other out and resulting in a loss of signal. Again with diversity systems, if one antenna loses the signal, the other will take over without any conspicuous break in the audio. In the event of poor reception, elevating a receiver or placing it closer to the transmitter is the best solution. Balcony locations are good since they can offer more elevation and unobstructed line of sight to the transmitters.

Since other **RF** (radio frequency) sources can sometimes interfere with wireless operation, receivers have a **mute** (or **squelch**) control that can be adjusted to reject "stray" frequencies when signal is lost or the transmitter is cut off. I find most squelch are adjusted properly at the factory, so it's not likely you'll need to worry about this. (I'll discuss other simple ways to address interference problems in the Troubleshooting section.) Other typical receiver features include indicators or meters for RF, to show transmitter reception, and audio, showing peaks or levels, plus *gain* or *level* controls on both transmitter and receiver. Also be aware that there are a few battery-operated receiver models designed for the freedom of camera mounting in video applications.

One other convenient feature showing up in UHF is a naming feature in LCD displays, convenient for "labeling" multiple wireless. If a system doesn't have a naming feature, I like tuning the displayed frequencies so the last whole number "labels" the unit, such as 761.000MHz, 762.000MHz, and 763.000MHz for wireless 1, 2, and 3.

Wireless **lapels** are "tie-clip" style mics used primarily for speaking and theatre, though they can also be effective for some creative micing including acoustic guitar and mobile percussion players (which I talked about in the last chapter). Lapel systems utilize a battery-operated beltpack module for the electronics and transmitter. Mics are available in omnidirectional and unidirectional models. Most people think that, as with hand-held mics, a unidirectional pattern is best for lapels because it is less prone to *feedback*[4]. However, due to the chest or head (in theatre) placement of lapel mics, there ends up being little difference in the feedback potential between omni and uni patterns but considerable difference in the way they perform.

Since unidirectionals are designed to reject distant and off-axis pickup to reduce feedback and background sounds, lapel placement ends up rejecting the voice as well, necessitating increased gain to restore vocal level. As a result, feedback potential is increased (especially in the higher frequencies) and the gain at the mic element itself can be up to three times louder than an omni in the same position. This makes the unidirectional mic much more subject to noises such as breath or wind, rubbing of clothing, or microphonic noise from the cable itself. (If you ever hear a pastor's broadcast with a lot of extraneous breath or clothing noise, you know the soundman made the mistake of using a unidirectional lapel.) A final problem with these mics at the chest location is a greater tendency to lose the voice when the user turns his head, another shortcoming of rejection. The solution: *use an omnidirectional.*

Wireless **handhelds** have self-contained transmitters in their handles, and **headworn boom** mics use a belt-pack module like lapel systems. Unidirectional patterns are typical for singing where more level and isolation is demanded for main and monitor speakers, but mic placement of headworns is crucial since slight changes in position around the mouth can alter the sound. Though there are quality brands by Audio-Technica, Crown, and Countryman to name a few, these hands-free mics have been

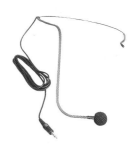

a bit of a problem for pastors and public speaking due to their conspicuous appearance. For these speaking applications, "near invisible" mini-earworn mics have finally arrived.

It has always made more sense for a public-speaking headworn to be omnidirectional like a lapel. There is little need for isolation from loud music, an omni element can be much smaller since it requires no unidirectional vents, and it suffers no proximity effect. It can be positioned at the side of the face so it requires no bulky windscreen to avoid breath pop and, unlike lapel mics, it follows the head movement at a much closer distance to the mouth. Before economical models were available, I made my first by wiring a small omni lapel element to an old headworn frame and painting it flesh colored. It cost me $100 and sounded as good as units over $500! But now we have affordable models such as the Countryman E6, Audio-Technica Microset (my favorite), and the Audix HT5, and I'm sure more will follow.

Lectrosonics and Azden were the first wireless companies to offer a small transmitter module that will plug into the base of any normal mic and turn it into a wireless. This design doesn't compromise the sonic integrity of the mic casing itself and gives you options on mic choices. I've even used wireless modules on miniature podium condensers for cable-free operation in the  middle of a floor, but the module either needs to provide phantom power or plug into a battery-operated pack designed to power the mic. If the module gain can adjust low enough to handle line-level signals (which I found most do), you can also provide wireless transmission for line sources such as a mixer to an amp rack or broadcast system in a portable application. (I once used a module to transmit from a sanctuary mixer to a social hall system in a church, but I wired the module to an appropriate AC adapter so they wouldn't have to worry about batteries.) In other words, wireless potential challenges us to be innovative.

TROUBLESHOOTING

Reception: The first concern with wireless setup is making sure you get strong and consistent reception of the mics. As I mentioned before, most single antenna (non-diversity) systems are dependable indoors within a 50' range and dual antenna (diversity) to a 75' to 100' range, in spite of the fact that some specs tell you they're good for 200 feet to 1/4 mile. Of course, this is under perfect conditions: the Bonneville salt flats on a clear day with no sunspot activity. (Frankly, I can't even recall the last time Billy Graham had a crusade there.)

I usually set up receivers at my mixer location so I can see the RF indicators and know when the transmitters are active, but there have been some situations where I placed receivers near the stage and ran their signals through an audio snake due to problems with space limitations, distance, or potential interference from digital audio or multimedia equipment at the mix position. The main concern here is having the extra lines from the stage and making sure they're **balanced**[10] connections either available on the receiver or achieved with a **direct box**[6].

Place receivers for maximum reasonable elevation, and make sure antennas are fully extended. Set one antenna vertical and a second angled, or experiment with antenna angles if you still have some dropout problems. Also, with many VHF belt-pack transmitters, the mic cable doubles as an antenna so make sure it is relatively straight and not bundled or coiled up while in use. I'll run you through a series of reception checks in the next section.

Interference: This stuff can be mysterious. Sometimes interference sounds like erratic distortion, noise, or static. Sometimes it sounds like mic feedback, though it's distinguished by multiple tones that fade in and out and are not constant like feedback. It can also result in momentary static when the transmitter is cut off, the effect of an instantaneous interference before the receiver has a chance to auto-mute after losing its signal. You would only notice this with *silent on/off* systems since many brands have an inherent pop when the transmitters are cut on or off.

In any case, interference is a point where the receiver is trying to receive another renegade signal from somewhere else, either when the transmitter's signal is lost or weak, or when the stray signal is just too strong on that particular frequency. Though it can be caused by other wireless, offenders include TV broadcast frequencies, power transformers, and digital equipment such as CD player/recorders, digital mixers, computers and digital video gear, keyboards, and effects units. I've also had situations where two wireless systems of different brands *and frequencies* interfered with each other, where a digital lighting board and CD duplicator caused problems with particular channels, and a system in a church at the other end of the block was picked up 500 feet away! If this occurs with VHF, it's probably time for a new UHF system with switchable frequencies, but there are a few preventatives or quick fixes to consider beforehand.

First, never buy a wireless system that transmits on local TV or DTV broadcast frequencies. (The stores should have a manufacturer's list of such frequencies.) It is really the responsibility of the wireless dealer and manufacturer to collaborate on providing only those systems that avoid local stations, and to make sure any multiple systems you might have or add are compatible. But you can avoid problems by raising the issue and making sure they don't sell you the wrong frequencies, and that you can swap a system if you have problems. VHF has offered some "traveling" channels that don't correspond to any broadcast stations, but switchable UHF is clearly better at this point for travel or otherwise.

The first step in determining interference problems is to power up systems without transmitters on and see if any of their RF meters indicate reception. If so, begin cutting off nearby equipment one at a time, especially digital equipment, to see if the RF indicator goes out. You may find that your CD player or reverb unit is causing the problem. Once the culprit is found, you've got a few and/or choices: move the offender or wireless farther away, switch frequency (UHF), adjust the mute control (if available) to the point where the RF indicator goes out, or drop adjustable-length antenna down one or two sections from the top. (This can act like a mute by weakening signal reception and, unlike mute, also works when the transmitter is on.) In the latter two cases, you just want to make sure the adjustment doesn't lose your transmitter signal, too.

Once outside problems are eliminated, it's time to check transmitters one at a time. As each one is cut on, take note if its signal is picked up on more than its own receiver (the RF indicator again). This can be caused by spur frequencies when transmitters are right by the receivers, and will typically disappear when the transmitters are farther away during normal use. If the problem doesn't go away, you have an incompatible unit and will have to switch frequencies or replace it. This is more common with older systems where frequency filtering may not be adequate. As a result, it is often better to stick with one manufacturer when combining multiple systems.

Once the transmitters are being properly received, check reception at your maximum working distance from the receivers. If you start getting dropouts, try eliminating them by checking batteries and antenna extension, adjusting antenna angles, making minor mute adjustments, or elevating the receivers. If this doesn't work, you may simply need to move the receivers closer to the transmitters. Except for larger systems and venues, I usually avoid the expense of going to external antenna distribution systems. Be mindful of the possibility for interference from nearby duplicate wireless if you are in a convention or meeting facility, near another church, etc. The unlikelihood of identical frequencies or sheer distance alone is usually sufficient insurance, but it is always wise to be ready for potential problems.

      Gain Settings: Setting proper levels with our gain and volume controls allows us to get a good clear signal without distortion. *Gain*[1] or **sensitivity** usually implies level *into* a device, where **volume** or **level** is output *from* a device. Transmitters have a sensitivity control in either an LCD display menu, or somewhere along the outside casing, or in the battery compartment as a recessed screw-type adjustment. But don't fret about having to make immediate adjustments because, most of the time, gains are set okay from the factory.

      Receivers have an audio level control for their outputs, and I normally want this setting all the way up for the strongest signal and lowest noise to my mixer. Most mixers have input gain control and peak level indication on each channel to let you know if a receiver signal is too strong. You'll need to adjust this channel gain to the point where the peak indicator does not illuminate during the loudest signals from the wireless. If your mixer does not have sufficient gain or **pad** control on the channel, you will need to back off on the receiver level adjustment if you notice distortion or mixer meters going into the red. (More in Chapter 6.)

      The sensitivity setting on the transmitter serves the same purpose. If the level is too strong, the signal will distort. Unlike the mixer settings, I can't make a quick transmitter adjustment once things get going, so I'll want to make sure this is properly set ahead of time. All you need to do is have the mic user speak, sing, or play at their loudest level and see if you notice any distortion in the sound or peak indication on the receiver. If not, leave the sensitivity at the factory setting. If you do notice distortion and it is not the mixer channel, simply lower the transmitter sensitivity until distortion ceases or the peak indicator doesn't light. For those receivers with an actual audio-level meter, adjust the transmitter sensitivity so the loudest signals just barely reach peak level. This will assure low-noise operation since some receivers exhibit inherent noise if mixer channels are cranked up due to a low transmitter signal. Check your owner's manual for specific adjustment details.

      Equalization: Recommending *EQ*[7] (or tone) settings for your wireless is a little touchy because it is dependent on the sound quality of your speakers and any corrective equalization of the sound system itself. I can offer some appropriate suggestions based on an accurate system, or which should at least get you headed in the right direction for those "I-hope-to-eventually-upgrade" situations. In regard to the following notes, I refer you again to Chapter 6 (mixers) for an in-depth discussion of EQ adjustments including **sweep EQ** which can be essential here.

      Handhelds are not much of a problem through a properly tuned system. Prime concern is the proximity effect of unidirectionals. When the user is more than 6 inches away, you can leave the low-end EQ control at the 11:00 to 12:00 position. *Do not boost low end for vocals because it can make the sound muddy or boomy.* As people get closer to the mic, you'll need to decrease the low end a notch or two more. The same applies for **headworn unidirectionals**, along with controlling some potential high-end "edge" from their smaller condenser elements. If this is too pronounced, you'll need to set the midsweep frequency somewhere between 3kHz and 6.3kHz (around 1:00 to 3:00 on most mixers), and back off its associated mid-gain control to the 11:00 or 10:00 position depending on how harsh the "edge" is.

  Lapel mics have always been more of a problem due to their off-axis location, requiring more level and EQ adjustment to pick up the voice clearly without feedback. Unidirectional lapels tend to sound thinner due to distance rejection (proximity effect in reverse), and will typically have more feedback problems in the high end from 2kHz to 8kHz. Unfortunately, EQ adjustments to take out this problem can also diminish vocal clarity in the same high-end ranges. This clarity is one of the most important aspects of lapel performance because, in many rooms, it works in conjunction with the natural projection of ambient low and low-mid sound from the voice itself. Without this clarity, the voice sounds muddy from a distance, lacking the supplemental detail necessary for everyone to hear clearly. So EQ accordingly for uni lapels without overdoing it and losing your clarity.

  Since omnidirectional lapels don't suffer from the gain loss or limited pickup due to rejection, their sonic surplus is in the lower frequencies which can be accentuated by the mic picking up chest resonance. (Put your ear to someone's chest while they're speaking and you'll know what I mean. This is best not performed on strangers.) As a result, we need to decrease specific low and low-mid frequencies which, fortunately, does not affect the clarity range. Depending on the user's vocal tone, I might start by backing off the low end to the 11:00 or 10:00 position to reduce muddiness while taking care not to make the voice sound too thin.

  The low-mid problem is around 400Hz to 600Hz which causes a "hollow" muddiness, is most prone to feedback, and which falls within the *room resonance* range of most facilities. This actually amplifies the problem and makes the sound even more muddy and reverberant. Reducing these frequencies not only clears up the sound, but diminishes its resonance in the room. I would start around 600Hz which is typically in the 10:00 to 11:00 range on a midsweep, and reduce the associated mid-gain control to the 10:00 or even 9:00 position. You can then re-adjust the midsweep back and forth a little if needed to the point where you get the least feedback and notice the sound being the clearest and most pleasing. Once these ranges are under control, you should have some room to bring up high end if necessary. Some lapels may require a little boost, especially around 2.5kHz which can help increase level and clarity on a soft or muffled voice.

  Obviously, this can be a problem if you don't have midsweep EQ, but I've found a way around this in smaller venues where the ambient voice is more prominent. Without the capability to address specific lower frequencies, we must increase the higher frequencies in an attempt to overcome the predominant lows. To accomplish this with 3-band fixed EQ, first increase the high end by one or two notches. Second, if you have a 1kHz mid (notated in the owner's manual specifications), back it off to about 10:00. If it's a 2.5kHz mid, you may need to boost it slightly. Finally, adjust the low EQ back if the voice still sounds a bit muddy. By just adding supplemental mic level with the natural voice, these settings should help achieve the clarity you need without feedback problems.

With **mini-earworn omnidirectionals**, you can adjust the same as for a lapel though you may not need the same degree of adjustment. Normally, you won't have to increase high end and the 400Hz to 600Hz gain adjustment can be a notch or two less.

Batteries: I once asked a major theatrical engineer if she used rechargeables for her shows. She said, "You don't trust a $10,000,000 show to anything but a fresh alkaline." Though most of you are probably not in a multimillion-dollar production, this advice may be appropriate to the importance you place on your task.

Where alkalines will give you at least ten hours on most newer wireless systems, rechargeables usually last less than half that and they can require following a strict regimen. Rechargeables, except for nickel hydride, can develop a memory if only partially drained for a routine period of time and then recharged. They will eventually lose their optimum working limit, dying at or before the end of the routine period. To avoid this, you must fully drain the rechargeable after its use before recharging. Also, some batteries don't reach full voltage. Some rechargeable 9V batteries reach under 8 volts max, and some wireless can start to have problems under 8 volts. I've even tested batteries which not only had short operating duration, but whose maximum voltage declined with each recharge. My choice is to stick with alkalines and find a good wholesale supplier.

It's best to check batteries with a voltage meter before you use them since even new batteries can sometimes be defective. Where most older wireless systems used 9V batteries, newer ones are gravitating to dual AAs which are getting up to fifteen hours on alkaline. If a used battery is down by 10 percent, it will still be dependable for a normal dress rehearsal or church service. If it drops below 10 percent, I'll toss it. Many UHF systems now have battery meters in the transmitter display, and at least one current system by Audix has it on the receiver as well (I love that). I also prefer it when pastors power their wireless on and off as needed to save on batteries, and this is where *silent on/off* avoids any distracting noises. This allows the pastor's channel to be up and ready so a soundman doesn't miss cues and force the pastor to learn sign language.

Another potential problem can be battery contacts. Be aware that batteries can be slightly different in size, so stick to one brand as much as possible. 9V Duracells, for instance, are shorter than most. So if you use a longer battery and then swap to a shorter one, the battery contacts may be pushed back a bit too far for good connection. Contacts can also become dirty or oxidized from humidity or perspiration, so clean them periodically with tuner cleaner or alcohol. (Some farsighted manufacturers offer gold-plated contacts to reduce this problem.)

This chapter has addressed most of the wireless considerations and problems I've come across and, hopefully, there won't be too many more popping up. Obviously, attention to detail minimizes the problems, but I still hold to one thought: if you don't need to be unplugged, plug. Wireless systems are an unparalleled convenience when you need the freedom, but cabled mics present less costs and concerns. Choose wisely. More under **Church Sound** and **Theatrical Sound** in chapter 13.

5. DOWN TO THE WIRE

CABLES[9]

Now we're concerned with sending our source signals somewhere, so let's briefly touch on the subject of cables and connectors. Always keep in mind that signals flow like water, in one direction. (And for you smart guys who bring up phantom power, I'll say it's like salmon swimming upstream.) We're dealing with two types of signal travel determined by the output and input connections of our equipment — *balanced*[10] and *unbalanced*. Storytime!

Imagine Mr. Guy Nice walking to the library when he gets followed by a large hissing, snorting bully. Once he reaches the serene environment of his destination, he has brought along a serious and uncontrollable deterrent to bibliophilic harmony. (You can look that up, 'cause I did.) Now imagine Mr. Nice meeting his younger brother at the library, both having been followed by bullies of equal stature and territorial tendencies. At the door, neither goon is willing to give way to the other and they commence in a spirited altercation, leaving the brothers and library patrons inside in perfect peace.

Now stick with me on this. The brothers are your source signals traveling down a cable, the bullies are noise, and the library is your signal destination. The first example is an *unbalanced* cable with noise picked up along its length and no way to keep it from "getting in the door." The second example substitutes a *balanced* cable with an added "neutral" signal. Once at the destination, the noise introduced to both lines cancels itself out leaving our desired signals undamaged. This is called **common mode rejection**. This is also called a **stretched analogy**.

Unbalancing Act: Unbalanced cables have two conductors: a **hot** (+) wire and a **ground** (−) or "shield" wire. The cable shield is wrapped around the hot wire to keep noise out, but there's a limit to its effectiveness. Noise is at relatively low levels, but gets stronger as it accumulates over a cable's length. **Signal-to-noise** will determine how much of a problem this will cause and what we can get away with. Remember when we talked about source levels and *gain*[1]? A microphone has a low level of around -60dB. If noise accumulates to -70dB over 100 feet of cable, it will be almost as loud as our signal. As a result, unbalanced high-impedance mics or low-level guitar signals can't be sent through long cables. But a +4dB line level from a synthesizer or instrument preamp through the same 100' cable would yield a 74dB signal-to-noise difference which can effectively mask noise. Such lines, therefore, could feasibly employ a longer run except for one other possibility — *ground loops*[11].

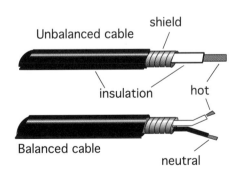

Unbalanced cable — shield, insulation, hot
Balanced cable — neutral

No, ground loops are not a new high-fiber cereal. They are hums caused by the signal cable ground of one *AC-powered* unit connected to another, more specifically when they're plugged into different electrical wall circuits. So we would have to break the signal ground somehow to eliminate our final connection problem, and you can't do it with an unbalanced line because it will cut your audio. The good news is that balanced lines can help eliminate both noise and ground loops.

Balancing Act: Balanced cables have three conductors as illustrated: a **hot** (+), a **neutral** (–), and a **ground**. The hot and neutral carry the actual signal, so the ground can be cut at one end to eliminate a ground loop if one appears. The rule is to cut it at the input or receiving connector of a device. Without even saying, "Abracadabra," all your noise problems will disappear and everyone will be in awe of your power. There have been occasions, though, when I was waiting for the applause and suddenly realized that the noise was still there. This could indicate a problem with equipment or cables, incompatible chassis ground designs, or inherent noise in the source or electrical lines (often caused by lighting dimmers on the same circuit). Beginning at sources, start cutting off or unplugging things one at a time and possibly switching electrical circuits to track this one down.

Another cute trick is eliminating a ground loop from an unbalanced output. As long as your destination is a balanced input, a cable can be made that connects the *hot* and *ground* of the output unit to the *hot* and *neutral* of the destination input with the same results because the ground of the input is not connected. More applause!

Direct Box: Unbalanced lines can be changed to balanced with a unit called a ***direct box***[6]. This is a $10 balancing transformer that sells for $40 because musicians are suckers. It normally offers two 1/4" phone jacks and an XLR connector. Plug the instrument into one 1/4", run a patch cable from the other to the instrument amp (if applicable), and a mic line from the XLR to the mixer. Most also have a ground lift switch to break a ground loop. A direct box is especially necessary with low-level sources such as bass or guitar, but should be used on any unbalanced sources having to traverse more than 30 feet of cable.

These connections are all used for mic and line sources, and require shielded cables. You'll also find a great deal of these in a single convenient package called a **snake** cable for running long distances. Speakers require larger gauge cables with side-by-side wiring and some unique connectors. I'll elaborate on them later in the amplifier chapter.

Auxes[13] – Now let's say we have an icemaker in the fridge. We hook a small tap and valve off the pipe under the sink and feed the hose over to the icemaker. We've just employed an auxiliary line to feed another device, just as a channel can send to effects or stage monitors. Such channel controls may be called **aux**, **effect**, **send**, **monitor**, or **foldback**. (The latter may show up on some older mixers.)

EQ[7] – Finally, we'll hook up an activated charcoal filter on the line to remove impurities from the water. Likewise, the channel **equalizer** section is a filter to control tonal "impurities."

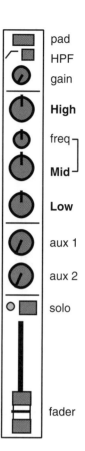

That's all the major channel controls. For each type of level control on each channel, there will usually be a corresponding master control such as Aux 1 master, Effect Send master, L-R/Stereo/Main fader, etc. The whistles will determine our flexibility in choosing how auxes are affected by other things on the channel, where we want to route our channel outputs, more EQ control, etc.

INPUT STAGE

Finally, we get back to that part about sources and levels at the start of the book. The proper mixer will provide the balanced and unbalanced input connections needed for your sources. Then the signal goes straight to the *gain*[1] control where we can accommodate all those great variations in dB levels. We'll bring up the gain control for those low-level mic signals, and bring it down for those hot keyboard signals.

How do we know when the setting is right? Most mixers have a channel peak LED that will light up red when the signal is too hot and might distort or damage something. While the source is playing (or singing) its loudest, bring up the gain until you see red. Then drop it back a notch or so and you're set. What if it's all the way down and you still see red? This may occur with hot signals like kick drum mics, so some mixers have a gain **pad** switch that will drop the level another 20dB or so, giving you more range to make your adjustment. If the mixer has channel **PFL** or **Solo** switches (see *Downtown* later in this chapter), they will typically route channel level to an indicated master meter for more precise display. Then simply adjust gain for a good meter reading. Check the owner's manual for specific details.

There will usually be *phantom power*[3] switching available somewhere, either as a global switch or on individual channels. This cuts on a 24 to 48 volt DC supply to the balanced XLR inputs for those condenser mics we spoke about. The (+) voltage travels down the hot *and* neutral wire, and the (–) voltage travels through the ground shield. A global phantom power will not affect dynamic mics, but *can be shorted by an unbalanced XLR cable with pin 1 jumped to pin 2 or 3*. (Don't use these!) Phantom power may affect some instrument preamps, but a direct box should eliminate the problem.

Other features can include channel **mute** (on/off) switches, **HPF** (**H**igh **P**ass **F**ilter) switches to reduce bass frequencies, and *phase reverse*[14] which can help if you have a few mics wired up backwards, or *out of phase*. I'll talk more about this when we get into some applications. Plus, it's 2 a.m. in the morning and I think *my* phase is getting a little reversed.

PRE/POST AUXES[13]

Let's go back to our ice-maker hookup. Tapped off the pipe under the sink, it will obviously be controlled by the input valve. It will not be affected by the faucet, therefore we'll call it "pre-faucet." If we could hook it up after the faucet, we would call it "post-faucet" and it *would* be affected. Likewise, if the tap is before the charcoal filter, it is pre-filter and impurities will not be removed from the ice-maker line. If connected post-filter, it will get filtered water.

The same goes for channel auxes. They can be tapped off the circuit **pre** or **post EQ**, and **pre** or **post fader**. (The owner's manual should illustrate which ones are which in a simple "map" called the **block diagram**.) The better mixers will often include pre/post fader switches so you'll have a choice. Generally speaking, stage monitor feeds are pre-fader auxes. This is so changes you make in fader level for the room sound won't alter monitor levels or cause potential feedback. However, I prefer post-fader auxes for many sources in church services since, unlike the typical concert, performers may be changing from week to week. Rather than constantly altering all the pre-fader monitor settings, it can be easier having good monitor settings that all adjust appropriately with my fader moves. If a singer is louder than last week's, I bring them down on the fader and they drop proportionately in the monitors. Same in reverse for a soft singer. As a result, balancing the house sound simultaneously balances all the monitors.

Post-fader is also preferred for accompaniment soundtracks. If the song is a bit too soft in the beginning, a fader increase for the congregation reflects in the monitors so performers can cue off the music better. If it's a live-performance track that needs to be faded in or out, this will also fade the monitor feed. (A pre-fader aux would allow the music to continue blasting through the monitors after the house sound is faded.)

To provide flexibility in these instances, it is best when a mixer has pre/post switching on *every* channel for aux singles or pairs. This allows me to select the primary vocal leader and instrument channels for pre-fader monitor sends as needed. Though some mixers have pre-fader auxes that are pre-EQ as well, they should be post-EQ so that any essential tonal adjustments will be reflected in the monitors, too. Effects feeds are post-EQ/post-fader auxes to allow the effects you add to follow the original signal in tone and balance.

EQUALIZERS[7]

Many people use EQ like Renuzit air freshener. Something stinks, so they start adding stuff to try to cover it up. You can find these people by looking at their EQ knobs; all the notches will be pointing to the right side. If something stinks in my house, my solution is to get rid of the problem first. (Then I don't have any socks to wear!)

When you're listening to a sound, don't think about what it's missing. Think first about what it's got too much of. This was the basis for my previous drum and wireless-lapel EQ suggestions. If a drum or mic sounds muddy, most people would probably try to cover it up with an abundance of high EQ. This creates frequency peaks that are harsh and prone to feedback. Better to eliminate the muddiness first, then add subtle amounts of high end if needed. In other words, use both sides of the EQ knobs. I typically cut 80 percent of the time. Before we start turning knobs, however, let's find out what we're controlling when we do.

Hertz: Tonal frequencies are designated in **Hertz** (**Hz**), or cycles per second. The audible range is 20Hz to 20,000Hz (20kHz, or *kiloHertz*). Below is a graph describing the various frequency ranges along with their positive and negative characteristics. (I hope you appreciate the brilliant terminology.) This should be a valuable aid in learning how to pinpoint and control your equalization.

+ / –	Demolition? Subsonic	Tight kick Boominess	Fullness Muddiness	Warmth Hollowness	Definition Harshness	Clarity Piercing	Brightness Edgy/whistley	Brilliance Sibilance
	L	O	W	M	I	D	H	I	G	H

20Hz   40Hz   70Hz   200Hz   500Hz   2kHz   5kHz   10kHz   20kHz

From the preceding graph, you can note particular sonic characteristics you need to control and adjust accordingly. Following are some more tips and information:

50–70Hz: The chest-resonant range where you feel tight kick. Too much is boomy and wastes watts.

100–250Hz: There are usually muddy problems to take out here, but can also be used to add fullness to a "midrangy" sound.

300–500Hz: Adds warmth to a thin sound. Too much causes a hollow resonance which can be accentuated by large rooms.

500–2kHz: Critical midrange region for most sources. Cut if sound is harsh or "nasally."

2kHz–5kHz: Guitar edge, drum attack, vocal presence, etc. Ear's most sensitive range, so don't overdo it. Cut if sound is piercing.

5kHz–10kHz: Can add brightness, but too much is prone to a brittle or whistley sound. Electronic hiss is typically above 8k.

10kHz–15kHz: Cuts excessive sibilance, or adds sweet-sounding highs on vocals, cymbals, string instruments, etc.

EQ Features: Your stereo hi-fi probably has a bass and treble control. This would be **2-band fixed EQ**. The same shows up on the most basic mixers. These are typically **shelving** controls, boosting (to the right) or cutting (to the left) a broad "shelf" of frequencies at 100Hz and below for bass and 10kHz and above for treble. Each notch is a subtle change in the frequency level and straight up (or 12:00) is **flat**, or no change. Some units also have a mid control centered at around 1kHz-2.5kHz. It's called a **peak & dip** control because this EQ curve acts as a boosted "hill" or cut "hole" shape centered around the set frequency. So, what if we want to change 500Hz? What if there's *feedback*[4] at 5kHz? We've got a bit of a problem because our mid-range control isn't fixed at those points.

Enter **sweep EQ**. In addition to our mid-range gain knob, there is an adjacent *frequency* knob that allows us to vary a whole range of mid frequencies. Now our mid range isn't limited to a fixed point,

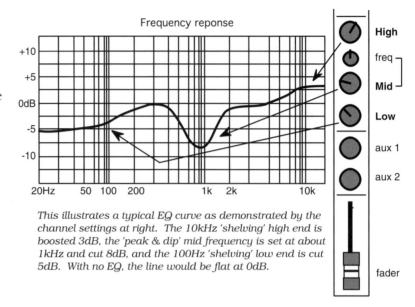

This illustrates a typical EQ curve as demonstrated by the channel settings at right. The 10kHz 'shelving' high end is boosted 3dB, the 'peak & dip' mid frequency is set at about 1kHz and cut 8dB, and the 100Hz 'shelving' low end is cut 5dB. With no EQ, the line would be flat at 0dB.

but will sweep from say 200Hz to 5kHz. Now I can set it at 5kHz and cut down the mid-gain control to get rid of that feedback. Even if I've got feedback I can't pinpoint, the sweep will help find it. I just set the mid gain at about the 10:00 position and rotate the corresponding frequency knob until I hear the feedback dip or stop. The same can be done for a muddy sound. Rotate frequency until the mud is gone. Then fine adjust the mid gain to take out only as much as you need to. Frequency found. Problem precluded.

This EQ configuration would be called **3-band w/sweep mid**. A better board might have **4-band w/dual sweep**, or a sweep on all the frequencies. Add a **"Q"** (width) adjustment and you get **parametric EQ** where you can set how broad a range of frequencies are affected by each sweep. The better the EQ, the more flexibility and ear training you'll get.

Tone Tips: Now that you understand something about EQ, it's safe to assume you should start making major adjustments to all your sources, right? WRONG, bandwidth breath! A speaker system with accurate response will eliminate the need for excessive tonal adjustments. Sources such as CDs, keyboards, properly mic'ed acoustic instruments, and vocals should require little or no EQ. Some sources that usually require more conscientious adjustment are close-mic'd drums and piano, instrument pickups run direct, and choir, lapel, and podium mics. Some more techniques will be touched on in chapter 10.

BUSSES & GROUPS

Just as the term seems to imply, **busses** are the lines that transport our channels "downtown" to the master section. If there is only one buss line running, you will only have a single channel level control. If there are two buss (or stereo) lines, you will also have a *pan*[15] control which can be adjusted to send the channel to the Left or Right output or any combination of the two. If there are more than two buss lines, there will be a L/R switch plus additional **assign-**

ment switches such as 1/2, 3/4, etc. to select which pair(s) you wish to use. (Some mixers have individual switches for each buss.) The pan will again be adjusted to send to the odd- or even-numbered assignment: pan left for 1 or 3, pan right for 2 or 4, and so on. There will be four or eight assignable busses, and several reasons for them. One is to send one or more assigned channels to a multitrack recorder via buss output connections. For example, with eight buss outputs on a mixer, I can connect directly to all inputs of an 8-track studio recorder. Then I can send any mixer channel to any track I want to record on by just assigning to the appropriate buss.

Another use is **channel grouping** used more in live applications. It's the reason busses are also called *groups*[16], and all these groups can be routed to the main outputs. There are many times when it's nice to have a single volume control for a whole bunch of specific channels. In the case of multiple drum mic channels, I can assign them all to group (buss) #1, then press a switch (usually just above the group fader) that routes that group to the L/R output. Then if I wish to control the drum level, I can simply adjust the #1 group fader instead of six channel faders at once. (I wouldn't want to strain myself.) Accordingly, I can assign other groups for multiple channels of background vocals, choir, orchestra, rhythm section, etc. If you're using a group assignment for a channel, don't forget to unassign the L/R (or Main, Mix, whatever it's called) switch on the channel so it's not going through both at the same time. That defeats the purpose.

*(Note: Be aware that major live sound mixers utilize **VCA grouping** which is different. Though they look like regular group faders, a VCA (voltage-controlled amplifier) is actually a sophisticated remote control of the selected channel levels themselves. In this case, you press an assignment button like normal grouping but leave the channel L/R switch on since that is the only switch that physically routes the signal to the main output.)*

DOWNTOWN

In the master section we'll at least have a few extra inputs, master controls for everything coming off the channels, and level meters. Main outputs go to the speaker amplifiers and any stereo recorders, aux outputs go to effects units or stage-monitor amplifiers, and group outputs can go to a multitrack recorder (if any). Live sound consoles may also have **matrix** outputs. These are simply "auxes" for the group and L/R busses rather than the channels. They can be used if you wish to send a simple group mix to another location.

Headphone outputs and control room (CR) feeds on recording consoles will allow you to monitor various outputs as well as individual channels via Solo buttons. As the name suggests, **Solo** will send one selected item alone to the headphones for your scrutiny. Such buttons may also be called **Cue** or **PFL** (pre-fader listen), or **AFL** (after-fader listen), which is the same as Solo. The difference is that Cue or PFL will allow you to monitor a source with its fader level off while Solo or AFL reflects actual fader settings and stereo pan positions. For the most part, PFL is preferred for live sound and AFL for recording. Some mixers will allow you to switch between both.

The extra inputs I mentioned will be *effects* or *stereo returns*[17]. They're actually the same as other channels except that they lack most of the features such as XLR mic inputs, EQ, or auxes. You will need to refer to specific mixers as to what they offer in their master package.

Levels: The most important point I can make here is not to overdrive your mixer outputs. Your meters will let you know what's going on. Set all your master levels at *unity gain*[2], which is usually represented by a "0" or thick mark on most controls. If in doubt, set master faders at two-thirds and knobs at halfway. Adjust individual channel levels as needed. Meters should hit at 0dB to +3dB maximum. If your system still isn't loud enough, your equipment levels are mismatched or you need additional amps and speakers. More later in the amplifier chapter, "Power Tools."

RECORDING MIXERS

The things that make recording most different from live sound are the controlled environment, a conceptual approach to the recording process (covered in Chapter 12), and the mixer. While all mixers have essentially the same features, one thing sets recording mixers apart — **track returns**. In live PA, we are dealing with a single-stage process. The sources come into the mixer and are sent out to the speaker system. In multitrack recording, it's a two-stage process. Sources come into the mixer and out to recorder tracks, then back from the recorder to the mixer track returns, which feed the speaker and headphone monitoring systems. These returns are additional channels that allow us to independently monitor tracks during recording or playback while the main channels are being used to send sources to the tracks. Most analog recording consoles are "in-line" designs with dual inputs and controls, for a channel and a track return, on each channel strip. A special switch can "flip" the tracks from the more basic returns over to the feature-packed main channels when it's time to mix everything down to stereo.

Other standard features on a recording mixer are **direct outputs** for sending individual channels to tracks, separate stereo studio and control room outputs, a talk-back mic assignable to studio or recorders, and stereo 2-track returns for the mix-down deck. Refer to specific manuals for hookup and available features.

Occasionally, you may find a need for additional inputs, or routing of signals and equipment, or both, especially in the studio. **Patchbays** and **mic preamps** are external devices that can expand on the capabilities of almost any mixer system. Though current I/O (Input/Output) capabilities on mixers, especially digital, have rendered patchbays nearly obsolete, I thought you should at least be familiar with their legacy.

Patchbays: As if you didn't have enough connections already, try adding a few hundred more! It may actually provide a convenience in some fixed installations, and you've already gone too far to turn back now. So when there are just too many input and output connections coming from all over the facility and behind your equipment, you can bring them all to one central, accessible spot — the patchbay.

All the desired gear hooks into the back of the patchbay, and can be designated with labels (or freehand scribblings for the meticulous) on the front. Whenever something needs to be connected to something else, we plug patch cords in the front from designated outputs to selected inputs. There are usually two rows of sixteen to twenty-four connections with a selection of RCA or balanced and unbalanced phone connectors available.

A **normalled** patchbay means it can already have over/under connections made for you internally. If, for example, an output like an aux send is hooked to a rear connection on the top row and an effects input is hooked up directly under it, the normalled circuit has already connected them so you don't need a patch cable. However, if you plug a patch cable into the front jack of either one, it disconnects them so they can be routed elsewhere. There's also **half-normalled** where only one of the over/under jacks will cause a disconnect (set primarily for input connections), and **parallel-normalled** where neither one will. Many patchbays have had switching for these various functions. This just makes it possible to expand and tailor a complex system to your specific needs.

Mic Preamps: These units offer basic balanced mic inputs, each with a separate direct output. Simple features include gain, phantom power, some kind of level or peak indication, and maybe phase reverse. No EQ, no auxes, no busses, no downtown. This lack of additional circuitry makes for a high-quality "straightline" design, so they're often used in studio recording for optimum sound straight to the recorder. They're available in solid-state and tube-circuit versions offering one to eight preamps in a single unit.

In addition to their studio appeal, they can be useful in live remote recording. Three 8-channel mic preamps like those by Presonus or Grace Designs offer 24 inputs and outputs for 24-track recording in a few spaces of an equipment rack. Many now offer internal analog-to-digital conversion for direct digital input into today's multitracks.

PROCESSOR CONNECTIONS

Chapters 9 and 10 will be devoted to external effects and signal processors, so let's talk about how these are connected to the mixer. We'll discuss two types of hookups: **direct** and **sidechain**.

Direct: Signal processors include units such as equalizers, compressors, noise gates, noise reduction, etc. The purpose of these is to process the whole signal to achieve the desired result. One way of doing this is to plug a source straight into a compatible processor, then out of the device to wherever you're going. Another method is using mixer *inserts*[12].

Inserts are **send and return** connections that are available at several points along the mixer's signal path. They will usually be on every channel, allowing processors to be easily hooked to individual sources. They can also be on groups or main outputs so you can process several things or everything at once.

Most inserts use a **1/4" TRS** phone connection, but not for a balanced function as we learned in the Input stage. Though configuration may vary, the **T**ip is usually the return from the processor and the **R**ing is the send to it. The **S**leeve is the common ground as always. When the plug of an **insert cable** is pushed into the insert, it automatically disconnects the mixer circuit at that point so the signal has to go through the processor and back. The other end of the insert cable has two separate connectors corresponding to the send and return; these plug into the processor input and output respectively. (If you're plugged in with processor on and no signal is flowing, you probably just have the connections backwards.)

If your mixer manual indicates that the insert Ring is indeed a send, you can also plug a mono 1/4" connection in halfway to get a pre-fader direct out without disconnecting the internal jumper of the insert jack. This allows you to feed the line-level signal of the inserts to multi-channel recording or monitoring systems without affecting your mixer channel operation.

Side-Chain: Unlike a signal processor, an effect such as reverb or echo is an embellishment to the original signal. It doesn't need to be processing the whole signal, just added to it. Accordingly, it is normally connected to an *aux*[13] output which sends its "side" signal to the effect input, then the effect output is patched to an *effects return*[17] to be added to the mix. Since most channels have control to this aux output, the effect can be added to any one of them. Also, a regular channel can be used as an effects return if you need the added features of EQ, pan, or monitor and recording sends for the effect. Just don't loop an effect through itself by inadvertently bringing up the aux send on its own return channel.

Another point is that effects units have a **balance** or **mix** control. This determines how much original signal is mixed in with the effect. In a mixer side-chain hookup, we already have original signal passing straight through the mixer so we don't want it coming through the effects unit again. So set the mix control *all* the way to "wet," "effect," 100 percent, whatever your unit calls it. (That terminology thing, again.) If you choose to run a source directly through an effects unit or patched through an insert connection, you'll need to adjust the mix control for the desired blend of original and effected signal.

Now, take everything you've just learned about mixer features and multiply it times three, throw in an extensive patchbay system, add all the effects and signal processing you'll learn more about in coming chapters, digitize everything in software and put it in a fancy-looking package, add plenty of controls and input/output connections, give it a memory and a mind of it's own (whoa, we're getting scary now!), and you'll have the wonder of... *(yeah, this means turn the page)*

7. VIRTUAL PLUMBING 201

AN INTRODUCTION

Well, hasn't digital technology just blown wide open! In addition to the boom in internet and handheld communications technology, digital mixers and recorders have made affordable world-class performance and features available to the masses. What gives digital products this potential for superiority? Let me offer a simple illustration:

An architect in Virginia prepares artwork of a house for a fellow architect in California. Once finished, he makes a copy of his final draft and faxes it out to his associate. As you can imagine, a good bit of quality and detail will be lost in the transition by attempting to pass the original through this "analog" process.

On the other hand, let's say the same architect opts to print an extensive list of instructions describing exact dimensions, angles, features, Pantone colors, etc. of the drawing. He makes a copy and sends a fax. Even if only barely readable, his associate can redraw a perfect version from the instructions. This is the "digital" process.

In digital audio, the sound is turned into digital instructions (1's and 0's) by an **analog-to-digital (AD) converter**. When it's ready to be retrieved for analog reproduction (such as with amps and speakers), the digital info is "redrawn" to analog form by a **digital-to-analog (DA) converter**. Result: a beautiful picture! With recording media, we are dealing with this basic process as a means of simply storing the original picture. With mixers and other audio equipment, however, converting to digital gives us a unique environment for accurately and efficiently manipulating the picture in almost any way imaginable.

Digital Domains: The thing that never ceases to amaze me is that the sounds we hear can be represented by a single waveform (or two for stereo). And from that waveform, which a speaker or headphone is reproducing with sound pressure changes as it moves back and forth, our magical ears can distinguish anything from a solo acoustic guitar to the collective instruments of a 60-piece orchestra. It is this complex waveform that the mixing or recording process must capture accurately.

In the digital domain, we can see this waveform picture as a graph. The vertical graduations are represented by the **bit resolution**. 16-bit means we have sixteen numbers and two possibilities for each number, a 1 or a 0. The total number of possibilities are 2^{16} or 65,536. The horizontal graduations are represented by the **sampling rate**, usually 48,000 times per second. So for each 1/48,000th of a second, we can put a dot on one of over 65,000 vertical points to plot our waveform—pretty fine detail if you ask me. And if we go to 20-bit technology, we'll have over 1,000,000 vertical points to choose from! This means an even smoother drawing with more dynamic range (the amount of headroom we have available for level from our softest to loudest passages). All in all, the higher the resolution, the clearer and more accurate the reproduction. At this printing, we've seen digital audio get to 32-bit/96k-sampling and some processing to 56-bit!

Why am I telling you all this? So you'll have a little better understanding of the technology that's permeating every aspect of audio — mixers, recorders, effects, and signal processors. Who could have imagined a decade ago that today you could have the capabilities of a $100,000 analog theatre console in a $2500 digital mixer, or a complete digital multitrack recording and mixing system for the same price? (Nostradamos said nothing about it.) In addition, digital allows the implementation of internal software-based audio components that duplicate sophisticated external units costing thousands of dollars, putting complete audio systems in one package and eliminating associated cable integration which can add to sound degradation.

The first time I started using a digital mixer in a studio after a decade on analog, I found myself still unconsciously bound to engineering techniques based around the limitations of analog. Suddenly I stopped, pushed myself away from the console, and sat a bit stunned realizing that I now had unlimited potential sitting in front of me. I was going to have to consciously clear my mind of all the self-imposed confinements of past technology and let my imagination soar. That is the first step in using digital mixers to their full potential.

For the same reasons computer-based video systems have replaced overhead and slide projectors, digital mixers now bless us with capabilities inconceivable with analog systems, at least for budgets under those requiring congressional approval. Yamaha was the first to introduce affordable digital mixers like the Promix 01, 02R, and 03D in the mid-nineties, establishing a new precedent in mixing technology. These were followed several years later by offerings from Tascam, Mackie, and a few others. In the future, we will see most (if not all) mixers resorting to digital technology due to its overwhelming advantages. That's what we're going to cover in this chapter. For most of you die-hard analog users, you're eventually just going to have to adapt. For all of you new to sound and starting on a digital mixer, anything less will seem like the "Stone Age."

Since you've just been through a mixer primer, I'll proceed into sections that echo those of the last chapter so we can cover the expanded features inherent to digital mixers. While most economical versions up to now have been designed with both live and recording use in mind, we are seeing a continuing split to more specific models for live sound. I'll be basing most of my discussion on Yamaha mixer features and terminology since the variations can be endless. Though these may differ from current products offered by other companies, including upscale commercial studio systems, Yamaha set the standards for affordable digital and you'll likely run into more of these than anything else.

EVERYTHING *AND* THE COMPUTER LINK

We have all the same basic elements as analog, just a lot more as you'll soon learn. But you will notice that digital mixers don't have as many knobs as an analog. For one thing, this keeps size manageable since a digital could have at least three times as many knobs for all the added features. (Think about that if you ever see a Yamaha 48-channel PM5000 analog and your head will be spinning.) It also keeps price down by avoiding literally hundreds of costly software-controlling encoders on the mixer surface. Instead, digitals offer a combination of faders and knobs that can switch to other functions along with on-screen control and lots of valuable information in the fancy LCD display. One distinct advantage here is that the clueless have less knobs to fiddle with while the competent are encouraged to know more about the ones they do. That can mean better engineering for everyone.

Faders – Digitals save cost and space with **motorized faders** and **fader layers**. A mixer may have only sixteen channel faders, but will have thirty-two actual channels available. A button somewhere will select channels 1-16 (on the first layer) or 17-32 (on a second layer). Some larger digitals may have twenty-four faders and a third layer for even more channels. Since the faders are motorized and digitally remember their settings, you will see them move to the settings for each layer you select. Any adjustments you make only affect the selected layer, and any changes will be retained as you switch through other layers. In live sound, I prefer to have all my channels available simultaneously. In the spontaneity of the moment it can be confusing knowing which layer you're on, so live digitals are incorporating more faders for minimizing or eliminating fader layers. We'll cover some other features of motorized faders in the next few sections.

Thanks For The Memory – As I said, the fader settings on a particular layer are retained as you move through other layers, and most mixers will remember your temporary adjustments even if you lose power or switch the unit off. But to change from this temporary buffer memory to permanent, we will need to store the settings in **scene memory**. This is a menu of numerous memory locations for naming, storing, protecting, and recalling complete mixer configurations including all your levels, aux settings, EQ, panning, processing, routing, and external digital interfacing and control parameters. In the recording studio, I can have different scenes for different songs and even varied mixes of those songs. For a church sound system, I can have stored settings for services, rehearsals, concerts, weddings, day-school programs, etc. Even if someone has messed with all my controls, I can press one or two buttons and everything is perfectly reset and ready to go. A school teacher who knows absolutely nothing about mixers can be trained to push those same buttons and activate perfect sound for her kids. You can't beat that for convenience and consistency. There are also individual memories for EQ, compression, routing, and more, which I'll talk about in their respective sections.

INPUT STAGE

We'll find the standard mixer input and output connections available, and an analog input circuitry to establish levels prior to the AD converter, which changes the signal to digital for the rest of its journey. There may also be channel *inserts*[12] so that external analog processing can be patched into this pre-digital circuit. We still have a *gain*[1] control, *phantom power*[3] on XLR inputs, and possibly a **pad** switch, typically the only non-memorized settings, though newer consoles are incorporating digital control of these as well. Beyond this, everything becomes software based including the **HPF** and *phase reverse*[14], and can therefore be stored in memory.

PRE/POST AUXES[13]

All limitations disappear here. Even the smallest Yamaha mixer at this printing has eight auxes, and all have individual pre/post switches for each channel plus flexible routing to any output connector *or* any effects units built into the mixer. This means you can have an aux routed to any of four to twenty-four standard aux output connectors (depending on mixer model), digital and analog main outputs, or any optional output cards that can be added to the mixer. You can even route a single aux to multiples of these outputs if you need the same mix to several destinations. All of the above aux controls are available on AUX (or SEND) pages in the digital screen, and the routing control is typically available on an input/output PATCH page.

The level control for aux sends is more graphic on a digital. The advantage of faders for channel levels is to make it easier to control multiples (try turning more than two knobs with individual fingers), and to provide a better visual reference of the levels. So imagine if we had enough funds and real estate to equip an analog mixer with faders for all our auxes as well. (We'd need a shuttle to get around the board!) With digital, we have two things that make this feasible: **motorized faders** that move to preset positions, and **fader layering** that can activate different functions. Now you can simply touch an aux button and your channel faders turn into those aux levels, making it much easier to see at a glance where all the levels are set. If you wish to bring up piano on the lead singer's Aux 1 monitor, press the Aux 1 button (you'll see the faders automatically switch positions) and bring up the piano fader. Simple. No hunting for a row of aux knobs or trying to see where each is set. When you're finished with adjustments, press any button other than an aux to get back to your main channel level layer.

There are a few other ways to control aux levels on most mixers. After the sound check and when I'm into a live performance, I prefer to keep faders in the channel level mode for house control and adjust monitors as needed through separate dedicated controls. Some mixers may have an encoder knob available above the channel fader that is  switchable for various auxes, or a "Selected Channel" area with either individual aux-level knobs or a single knob with a bank of aux-select buttons to make adjustments. Another method is on-screen in AUX or CHANNEL VIEW pages. These pages will allow you to see settings for the channels which can be adjusted either by *touchscreen* control, or by a row of "soft knob" encoders under the screen (so-called because their function changes according to adjacent on-screen designations), or with a data wheel and navigating cursor buttons on the mixer surface. All this means is that you have a few ways to make adjustments that suit your own engineering style or situation. As with any mixer, your preferred methods will soon become second nature.

EQUALIZERS[7]

On today's analog mixers, we've been fortunate to have 4-band with dual-sweep EQ available without breaking the bank. But we're more fortunate to have 4-band, full-parametric EQ on digitals that puts those to shame. Where the previous offers six knobs of control, the latter offers twelve. And digital EQ is much more precise. I first discovered this when the parametric EQ in a digital board outperformed a high-end analog 31-band graphic EQ for tuning subwoofers. As a result, I rarely use analog graphics anymore.

Digitals typically have a single set of dedicated EQ knobs, and you simply select a channel to make the adjustments. Some analog engineers would claim this is more complicated, but it's not really. Both are a 'three-stage' process. With analog, you (1) move to the channel, (2) move up the strip to the specific EQ control, and (3) turn the knob. With digital, you (1) press the channel's SELect or EDIT button, (2) move to the dedicated EQ band in the Selected

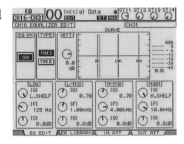

Channel section (sometimes this means pressing a band button), and (3) turn the knob. A couple of things that can make the digital more convenient is that one hand can remain in the same EQ area as you select different channels for adjustment, and you can see more precise EQ parameters and even the EQ curve itself in the LCD display. Did you ever wonder what frequency that analog sweep knob was on when it was at 1:30? Now the digital tells you it's exactly at 1.68kHz. As you hear that change and see the curve, you're actually getting advanced ear training for free!

Digitals don't just have EQ on the input channels — they normally have it on all the outputs as well. Now I can fine-tune mains and monitors or my overall recording mix with internal parametrics or, in the case of advanced models, internal graphic EQs. You say a 4-band parametric won't work in place of a graphic for tuning a room? That may be true with really bad speakers but with good speakers and a room of moderate size, I need only control three or four problem areas as the norm. I find that the digital parametric gives me precise and sufficiently flexible control for many venues, and eliminates the need and cost of external EQ and integration. (We'll discuss some external digital processors in chapter 9, Signal Corps.)

The convenience of individual memory functions starts here. Any specific EQ adjustments we set for a channel or output can be stored in an **EQ library**. This will be a menu on an EQ page where you can name, store, and recall various EQ settings. For example, if I have sixteen matching wireless lapel systems for a theatre production and I wish to start with a usable EQ setting for all of them, I can set that EQ on a channel, select and store it into the library as "Lapel," and then recall "Lapel" on every channel with a couple of speedy button pushes each. This latter step would take about five seconds total. (Try that on an analog!) Or I can move that mic to another channel and recall its EQ instantly. *BUT*, there's another library I prefer for that. You should also have a **Channel library** available (it's in the VIEW function on many Yamaha mixers). Settings in this library store all the channel parameters at once including EQ, fader and monitor levels, pans, compressor settings (which we'll get into shortly), routing... you name it. Now if I have similar channel sources or move a source elsewhere, I'll use this to transfer all the settings at once.

My standard procedure for organization's sake, and after I've set up all the channels on my mixer, is to go through each channel library spot (there's usually at least 100 memories) and store each consecutive channel in order. This gives me a backup of each individual channel named and numbered for its proper place in case I ever have to quickly restore a channel. Though I've never had a Yamaha digital mixer fail in over ten years of use, I still back up all of this memory data via computer software, MIDI data filer, and/or direct jumpdrive port (if available).

BUSSES & GROUPS

Most digital mixers have the same eight assignable busses found on larger analog mixers, and *pan*[15] controls to select left/right and odd/even outputs. The eight busses can again be used to send signals to a multitrack recorder or other destination, but the digital will give you options as to the quantity and type of buss output connections you prefer. (We'll cover those shortly in the *I/O Options* section.) For *groups*[16], however, digital mixers get radical. Larger live-sound digitals use **DCA** faders. Remember VCAs from the previous chapter? DCAs (digital-controlled amplifiers) are really the same thing in the digital domain, serving as assignable remote controls for groups of channel levels.

What if your digital doesn't have DCAs? Then it will likely offer an alternate feature. The motorized faders can be physically linked by selecting multiple channels to a **fader group**. Then when you move any channel fader in the group, all the others magically follow it. Now any fader serves as a remote control for all the others. I can fader-group my background vocals, choir, drums, orchestra, etc. Okay, you smart guys might be saying, "What if I've set different levels for the various channels? If they all come down together, won't the lowest ones cut off first?" Initially, I would commend you for being perceptive enough to consider their relative levels. Then I would explain that digital mixers with fader grouping are "intelligently" scaled. If you get a chance to try fader grouping, set the channel levels at widely varying positions, link all the faders, and then slowly bring them down (using one fader, of course). You will see that the faders change relative position to maintain relative levels, and they all reach bottom at the same time! Yes, the digital designers were way ahead of you.

Along with fader groups, there are also **mute groups** so you can mute all selected channels in a group with the push of a single on/off button. Remember when I talked about realizing the potential at the beginning of this chapter? Hey, we're only just getting started!

DOWNTOWN

Central to the master area is an LCD screen that displays most of the information we need. As mentioned in the previous Aux section, there will be touchscreen, soft-button, or cursor and data-wheel control for making on-screen adjustments, and sometimes a connection for control with a standard computer mouse is available. Smaller digitals have a few dedicated knobs for controlling EQ and pan while larger mixers will have extensive controls for aux levels and signal processors as well.

Where very few analog mixers have a full meter bridge (showing levels for all channels and outputs), even the smallest digitals have HOME or METER pages that display any number of comprehensive meters for checking levels at any input or output, and you can select either pre- or post-fader points for indication. With pre-fader, I can check a channel input gain or make sure a channel is active before I bring up the fader and commit it to the house. With post-fader, I can balance background vocalists or other sources visually by setting their respective faders so that the meter levels are all relatively even. (Useful if the engineer has a tin ear.) Or I can simply see which of eight mics that guy is actually talking on so I can adjust the right one.

Digitals usually have headphone and studio control room feeds along with a 2-track (stereo recorder) input and level control for monitoring recording or playback. **Solo** buttons will again let us monitor one or more channels through headphones or control-room monitors, and you have a switchable choice of **PFL** or **AFL** soloing as with some analog consoles.

Usually you won't see external *effects returns*[17], but rather additional sterco line channels and return channels for internal effects. And unlike analog, these returns will normally have all the same features as our regular channels including 4-band full parametric EQ, all aux sends, and flexible routing.

PROCESSORS

Now we have to break a little from the format of the last chapter to cover unique extras in the digital environment. One of the greatest luxuries is an abundance of sophisticated signal processing giving us unprecedented control and eliminating the need for most external devices covered in the next two chapters. As I indicated previously, there are anywhere from two to eight internal multi-effects units that can be digitally "patched" to any aux or channel insert. These will provide everything from reverbs and delays to pitch shift and electric guitar effects.

Even more amazing is the inclusion of compressor/limiters on every channel and output. This can protect the whole system, maintain maximum desired levels for your recording or house sound, or automatically balance some sources such as background vocals. (At the end of this chapter, I'll give you a few tips for compressor settings that will get you started.)

Though digitals have parametric EQ on the outputs, larger live sound models are currently including up to sixteen graphic EQs that can be patched wherever needed. Along with all the other effects and signal processing, any settings and routing can be stored in libraries and scene memories.

I/O OPTIONS

A smaller mixer may come standard with sixteen input and six output connectors, but has thirty-two channels inside, eight auxes, and a potential for up to twenty-two outputs! What's wrong with this picture? Nothing's wrong, you're just experiencing **open architecture**. While keeping the basic system economical (you may only need sixteen channels), this allows flexibility for expansion. *Open architecture* means we can add a selection and quantity of connections that serve our particular purpose. If we

need ADAT or TDIF digital connections for pro recording gear, we can add it. If we need eight more inputs for wireless mics and eight more outputs for stage monitors, we can add it. If we need sixteen feeds to CAT5 output for an Aviom digital in-ear monitor system, we can add it.

Most digital manufacturers offer some version of **I/O** (**I**nput/**O**utput) expansion made by them or third-party companies. These can be plugged into available card slots to expand the system. A single Yamaha option card may add up to sixteen digital inputs and outputs or up to eight analog inputs and outputs. The latter could equip our 16-channel mixer with 24 channels and 14 analog outputs (6 standard + 8 card). The inputs can go to additional channels already available in the mixer, and the extra outputs can handle all eight aux sends.

There are also some third-party, add-on effects and signal processing available from time to time. Once these elements are added, we need a flexible way to patch them in, just like wiring up external gear.

Patching: Just as we used analog patchbays for flexible I/O patching of external components, digitals offer *virtual patchbays* for making all our internal input, output, and processor connections. In PATCH displays, any input can be routed to any channel, though you would normally keep these in order to avoid confusion. Outputs can patch to any available output connectors: direct outs from channels (selectable pre- or post-fader), aux sends, buss or main stereo outputs, and even insert sends. This includes patching for any I/O cards you add. And numerous patch setups can be stored in libraries so you can change the whole configuration in an instant and save it with scene memories. This patch memory may also include a naming function so you can name each input and output for on-screen display to help keep track of what's what.

Mic Preamps: At present, analog option cards have only offered line-level inputs and outputs. If we need to add more mic channels, we can still add 8-channel mic preamps connected to option cards. Prices range from under $200 for the SM-Pro PR8 to $2000 or more for a Yamaha digital or studio models like Grace Designs. As mixer technology provides even more standard inputs, outputs, and channels for less cost, we'll see less of a need for options such as this, but it's nice to know we can add them when we need to.

Recording Mixers: With all this I/O expansion and patching, just about any digital can serve a dual purpose as a live or recording mixer. Rather than requiring an in-line, dual-input design like earlier analog recording consoles, a digital allows us the flexible input patching to route sources to channels and out to a multitrack recorder (using virtual busses or direct outs), and recorder track returns to channels for monitoring and mixdown. Rather than having a single function "flip" switch, they have fader layers and can store multiple recording and mixdown configurations as needed for easy recall. And unlike the analogs which have limited features on their second row of in-line channels, all digital channels are full featured so you have optimum control for both sources and tracks, including scene memory for storing your mix as you add tracks and progress through the project.

Models designed more with recording in mind may also include **automix**, another memory function that receives timecode from an audio or video recorder and remembers adjustments you make to the mix while the recorder (and its timecode) is running. With multitracks, you can work on one channel at a time — fader moves, on/off switches, pans, EQ changes and scene changes — building your mix while the board memorizes each move you make. When you're finished, push a button and it automatically plays back your perfected mix in time with the music or other program material. Gone are the days of AMS (Analog Mixdown Syndrome) when three people with six hands and caffeine overdose make all-night attempts to get a big mix right.

External Control: Some years back, I had a church music director request direct control of the music instruments and vocal mics since they didn't have a regular sound engineer. (Sound was controlled by a small, preset digital mixer in a sound room 80' away.) This would have been a weird proposition for an analog system because she wanted control of the house at her piano (fortunately, she could hear house speakers from her position), and needed to remove this "split" control from the floor for other basic services. Have no fear, digital is here!

It was economical enough to add a matching digital at the stage, but I didn't need an involved multichannel audio interconnect between mixers. Instead, I fashioned a single **MIDI** (**M**usical **I**nstrument **D**igital **I**nterface) connection from stage to booth. MIDI is more popular as a control format for keyboards and sequencers, but has also been common on digital mixers for external control and data backup. Though MIDI has a 5-pin plug, it only uses three pins for standard functions. So two XLR to MIDI adapters can be easily constructed that allow a MIDI connection through a standard mic cable, and I've had no problem with such basic control through a single line in a 200' audio snake (no matter what the experts say).

Once the main mixer was receiving the remote's MIDI output, I used its *Control Change* page to set what parameters the remote could control which can include any fader levels, aux levels, EQ, on/off, etc. I simply programmed it to allow only level control of the music channels, not pulpit, altar, pastor's wireless, etc. I could have programmed it for control of monitor levels alone, or I could have used a smaller MIDI controller like a J.L. Cooper Fadermaster for limited control capabilities. I have also used a second digital mixer located in a video production room to remotely control a house console's aux send(s) feeding a recording mix to video and CDR out in a balcony! Again, the possibilities seem endless.

Now digitals are incorporating software control and standard computer interfacing so it is possible to control the house mixer with a wireless LAN laptop from any seat in the house. Or a touring engineer can walk in with a jumpdrive on his key ring that will plug into a digital mixer and download all his settings in an instant for a major concert. I even anticipate potential MIDI control options such as a small personal monitor remote for performers (like some current multichannel in-ear monitor systems) with channel layers that can be assigned to control a complete aux section on the house mixer. Maybe I'm just dreaming, but then a lot of my dreams have already come true.

Cascading: Occasionally, one may have to make a choice: Do we spend $7500 for a 24-channel digital or $5000 for two 16-channels? It may be a question of expansion limitations, adding on to a mixer you already have, or simply having more channels for less money. The 32-channel for 30 percent less is enticing, and more feasible since we can digitally-cascade two mixers to act pretty much as one.

Where major mixers may offer optional cascade plug-ins and interconnects for expanded multi-console capabilities, some smaller mixers may interface using standard digital audio and MIDI connections. For example, two Yamaha 01V96 mixers can have common audio for six aux sends, stereo outputs, and channel solos by cascading their onboard 8-channel optical and stereo digital coax connections, and they can select fader layers as well as store, name, and recall scenes simultaneously via MIDI communication.

This allows expandability to an economical 32-fader dual system with 24 mic/line channels, 8 stereo line channels, 8 digital effects, and card expansion for even more inputs and outputs. The introduction of the Yamaha LS9 made a mass market 64-channel/64-fader dual system possible. I'll prefer a single package first, but poverty is the mother of invention. (Did I say that right?)

DIGITAL TIPS

One of the most important steps with a digital is initial setup which includes proper routing of inputs and outputs, tuning the system for proper gain structure throughout, and setting compressors for controlling levels. Once set, the mixer will then do about 75 percent of the work for you. Though digitals are capable of endless parameter adjustments to suit your whims, I have found some easy and useful settings on Yamaha boards that may be applicable to your equipment and needs. These should provide a good starting point if you're not sure where to begin. There are also plenty of factory presets you can try if mine don't work for you.

Levels: All the digitals I've used offer a pretty hot output. Since -12dB became a standard for *unity gain*[2] on digital equipment meters (equal to "0" on analog meters), a full "0" reading on your digital meter exiting a +4dB output connector can mean an actual +16dB heading to your amps. So average levels on your channel meters should run between -12dB and -6dB, allowing extra room for peaks. Your internal compressor settings will keep the rest under control. Then just make sure your amps are set for a comfortable volume. Just to be safe, digital manufacturers often allow a little headroom above peak on the meters to avoid distortion but, unfortunately, you won't know how much that is. So you'll need to make sure you stay below the peak or only barely touch it on occasion.

I run individual channels closer to full level in multitrack recording for maximum resolution to tracks but, in live sound, most of my sources are going to be running lower so that, collectively, they will stay within good operating levels for the rest of the sound system. Though input gains are the primary adjustment, there are some unique features for controlling channel levels including additional gains (in the ATTENUATION or EQ displays) and compressor output levels (in the DYNAMICS displays).

If I have analog input gain knobs that are not memorized with scenes, I may choose to set as many gains as possible across the board at an equal (and non-peaking) level like 11:00 so that numerous users such as a ministry sound team can easily remember those settings. Then I can use the internal digital levels to fine-tune for specific channels. If a podium mic needs more level for distance pickup, I could crank up its compressor output. If I need less level for a hot keyboard signal, I could drop its attenuator in the EQ screen. This just allows for more flexibility in how you control and store your level setups, and the range of these internal adjustments can be as much as ±18dB.

Since master outputs have the same controls, I can set my Stereo output fader at full level and store those "hidden" internal gains at a lower level so others aren't accidently (or intentionally) cranking up the master fader to uncomfortable levels or feedback. In multitrack recording, if my mix is set but the overall level to CDR is a bit low, I can bring up and store an internal level for the master output without re-adjusting my whole mix. *(Note: Be aware than an internal gain change will be pre-compressor so it will affect compression, but a compressor output level is post-compressor so the compression effect will not change.)*

Fader Stuff: Grouping of the motorized faders on digitals might bring up a question. What if I have something like background vocals linked, but I occasionally need to alter levels for one or two mics on the fly? It would be a pain to have to switch to the GROUP display, disable linking, and make a change, so Yamaha came up with one solution (and there may be more out there). Just press and hold the SEL button of the channel to make your adjustment. This temporarily disables the link for that channel so it can be changed, then re-establishes the link once the SEL button is released. (You don't have to worry about this with a DCA since it acts as a separate remote control, and your individual faders are always free to adjust.)

How about some creativity with layers and grouping? Let's say I need to work with fader layers because I have a 16-fader digital equipped for 32-channel capability or a 32-fader equipped for 64-channel capability, and I need nine channels for drum mics alone. I can route all but the kick mic to eight second-layer channels, then I can route the kick drum to a channel on the first layer and link all nine faders together so I never have to switch out of the first layer to adjust the whole drum kit. *Plus,* I've saved eight channels on the first layer for primary sources requiring more independent control. In this manner, I can have any extra linked channels on another layer, or simply sources that can stay preset or rarely need to be changed.

Compressors: Due to cost and space considerations, we were never in a position to demand compressors on every channel with affordable analog consoles. Now it's hard to imagine not having them since they make our job easier and duplicate the level control we've been accustomed to in studio applications. Even if I have singers or an engineer who can't balance, a proper setting on compressors can hold vocalists to a good blend. I'll cover more compressor specifics in chapter 9. For now, here are some basic settings you can try:

Lead singers: Threshold = -10dB to -5dB, Ratio = 5:1, Attack = 10ms, Release = 100ms, Knee = 5, Output = 0dB. (If you need a bit more level, bring up the output.)

Background singers: same settings except Threshold is set 3dB to 5dB lower. (This keeps their collective level just under lead vocals.)

Instruments could start the same as lead singers, but change Kick drum and Bass to Knee = 2 or 3, Attack = 5ms, and Release = 10ms.

Pastor and other speaking mics: Threshold = -20dB to -10dB depending on their dynamic range. (Some may go from a whisper to a scream.) Everything else is the same as lead vocals.

(Note: Compression isn't normally necessary for live choir, piano, orchestra, and CD playback channels. Also, all compression should be assigned pre-fader so you will get consistent compression regardless of your fader level adjustments.)

Main output (recording): Threshold = 0dB, Ratio = 1.5:1, Attack = 30ms, Release = 87ms, Knee = 5, Output = +3dB.

In recording, you have to be careful to get a good mastering level without squashing the sound. CDR mastering units or software usually have a *normalization* function that compensates for maximum levels to disc. If you don't have this, the above parameters are a decent setting I discovered on Yamaha mixers because it can top off peaks with very subtle compression and give you a visual indication of when you've reached full digital level. To check this level, go to the Dynamics display for the Stereo out and you should see only minimal GR (gain reduction) meter indication when mix levels are good. Make any master level adjustments with the digital gain (or ATTenuation) for the Stereo master. Try it and see how it works for you.

Main output protection (live sound): Threshold = 0dB, Ratio = INF (infinity), Attack = 1ms, Release = 100ms, Knee = 4 or 5, Output = 0dB.

Stage monitors: Same as Main, but Threshold can be set as low as -10dB to control peaks.

Digital Effects: We've had digital effects units for some time, so these internal units simply operate in the same way and there are a lot of good factory presets to choose from. One useful practice in live sound when a good aux recording mix is desired is to assign one effects unit solely to that aux mix to simulate a natural room reverberation. Depending on how large I want the room to sound, I'll set the reverb time at 2-2.5 seconds, and any pre-delay and initial delay to around 50ms to provide depth and separation. Diffusion is 8-10 for a smooth and dense reverb. Other effects units can be assigned to both house and recording mix as desired. This is all controlled by selecting the effects return channel, turning the stereo buss switch (in the Routing display) On for house or Off for recording alone, and adjusting the recording aux level of the return as needed.

Scene vs Manual Control: Scene memory is an invaluable asset for saving and recalling numerous setups especially in studio production, but it should not be overused in live applications to the point of complicating things by attempting to circumvent our brain's greater capacity for spontaneous discretion. The digital still responds and should be used much like an analog.

In ministry and theatre applications for instance, scenes should be used to automatically get everything to a proper starting point, and then our ears will guide us through needed manual adjustments as the program progresses. When your program follows the same format on a daily or weekly basis, you don't need various engineers constantly storing new scenes for every program and even parts of a program. This can quickly lead to inconsistencies in performance, the opposite of what you'd expect from a digital mixer. The key to live digital mixing is maintaining a comfortable balance of automation and manual control. As with most things, keep it as simple as possible and let your ears guide the rest.

In theatre, I only need recalls for crucial scene changes and special effects. In my church, I have three regular scenes for three different weekend services. I don't need additional scenes for a particular solo or choir number. For those, I simply adjust the channel(s) like I normally would on an analog. I don't need a special scene for a singer's odd vocal tone. If they happen to be singing that week, I just go to the *Channel View* library and recall their special setting on the appropriate channel. If I only want the pastor's mic active for the sermon, I could store a single "Sermon" scene or simply mute the other channels. Remember, there are mute groups (or DCA mutes) so only a few button pushes can mute everything.

I do have a special choir scene when using eight mini-earworn wireless mics to supplement level and bring the choir more out front of full band and orchestra. The scene automatically sets all the normal stuff along with special levels and EQ for all the earworns, including a little heavier compression that maintains a better balance with the rest of the choir. When they're finished, I return to the normal service scene to de-activate all the wireless.

MOD POD

In the future, I expect to see economical modular designs for live sound that allow even more flexibility in building a system. A modular design means the actual mixer can be in a rack-mount box located at the stage (like an oversized snake box), and could be either pre-configured or programmed like a digital signal processor for any mixer configuration you choose. All sources would plug straight into the mixer box eliminating the need for costly and bulky multichannel snakes. Then the component that actually looks like the mixer with all the faders and knobs would, in reality, be a big "mouse" console with a digital link to the mixer box including a few send/return lines for sound booth sources and stereo recording feeds. If you needed more channels, you could simply add another box and the console would handle it without requiring additional cabling to the booth. You could also parallel the digital connect to a second console for stage monitor control, but it would again remotely control the auxes in the mixer box itself without audio splits.

Far-fetched? Nope, this technology became a reality with the Yamaha PM1D digital modular console used for major events around the world, and digital snakes are beginning to offer similar interconnect capability "out of the box." But something well under the PM1D's current $100,000 price tag would mean I could present such an asset to a budget committee without having a defibrillator handy. I think it's just around the corner.

8. CAUSE & EFFECT

Trying to discuss the current state of effects devices is like trying to track the federal deficit — five minutes later, you're out of touch and it's out of sight! Frankly, I don't relish my whole life becoming a successive parade of new-product learning curves. Give me at least a few meager minutes for coffee and Fox News.

Seriously, it is truly amazing the quality and flexibility of today's digital effects. But to be practical and avoid a section rivaling Tolstoy's *War and Peace*, let me just give *you* a few meager minutes of basic descriptions and tips on the more common ones.

DELAY[18]

This is considered a single repeat of an original signal, with the delay time designated in milliseconds. 10–40ms can fatten up a vocal, 40–100ms gives the slap-back effect of small to medium rooms (popular in the recordings of the fifties), and 100–250ms simulates larger-room delays. Longer times are not very natural short of the Grand Canyon, and would be used primarily for special effects.

In recording, I sometimes like to use a quality delay unit to stereo image a mono source. Just pan the original sound to one side, and pan an effect unit's 10–20ms delayed return of the source to the other making sure it is 100 percent effect with no original signal mixed in. You might notice something unusual, though. If they're both set to the same meter levels, the original side still sounds louder. This is called the ***Haas effect***[19]. If a separate delayed signal is within 40ms of the original, the sound will be perceived as coming primarily from the direction of the first signal. It fools your ears. We'll find out later that the Haas effect has a very useful purpose in large-room sound system setups.

ECHO

Delay with decaying repeats. Adjustments of **feedback** or **regeneration**, as the repeats are called, are usually in percentages. I only use 15–25 percent for smooth 200ms echoes with 3 to 4 repeats. I also prefer using quarter-note-triplet echoes in music, because they will be more noticeable between the beats without overdoing the echo level. (If you don't understand triplets, swallow your pride and ask a musician to explain it.)

REVERB[20]

Reverb is very short echoes, or multiple reflections, so numerous that they create a dense and continuous effect that gradually decays. Natural reverb times for a good concert hall are 2 to 2.5 seconds long. A **pre-delay** setting, which simulates the delayed wall reflection preceding reverberation in a large room, can be set for 50–100ms to give the reverb more depth and slightly distance it from the original signal for clarity.

There are different types of reverbs to simulate various room characteristics, namely **hall**, **chamber**, and **room**. Another more synthetic type is **plate**, a bright-sounding effect simulating the large metal-plate reverbs of yesteryear, and **gated** (or **reverse**) reverb with an abrupt cutoff of the decay as if shut down by a noise gate. This was made popular on drums by Phil Collins of Genesis, and short versions make for an interesting "dense-delay" effect. In popular-music production, I reduce the bass frequencies of reverb in varying degrees to avoid smearing the low end of the mix.

MODULATED EFFECTS

Chorus is a lush effect that delays and modulates a pitch around the original note. I don't favor it much on vocals, but it's really nice on instruments where it adds color and fullness. It can give 6-string guitar a sound similar to a 12-string. **Flange** (I call it chorus with an attitude) is a short-delay chorus regenerated through itself to produce a more radical and hollow-sounding effect. **Leslie simulation** is another chorus variation based on the Doppler effect of the Leslie rotating speakers used with the classic Hammond organs. A unique feature is the switched and gradual speeding up and slowing down of the modulation to mimic the motorized speeds of a Leslie.

PITCH SHIFT

This one is pretty self-explanatory. It changes the pitch of a note to a selected interval which stays constant, unlike chorus which modulates around the note. Coarse adjustment is in half step (semitone) note increments and fine adjustments are in percentages of a half step. With a fine adjustment of 10–15 percent, you get an effect similar to chorus but cleaner, especially for vocal, since it isn't waving around. Coarse adjustment on vocal tends to get you into a higher "munchkin" or lower "demonic" sounding effect.

I call this "stupid" pitch shift, because we also have **intelligent pitch shift**, also called **harmonizing**, which goes a step further. You can select a root key and a musical scale or mode, and the pitch will follow musical notes in specific harmony intervals allowing you to sing or play harmony with yourself! Units which have offered this include the Eventide Harmonizers, newer Yamaha SPX effects, and Digitech Vocalizers. In addition, there are high-quality, dedicated **pitch correctors** like the Antares that will correct pitch in real time. It's getting to the point where, if you can't carry a tune in a bucket, you can dump it from a pitch corrector.

There are many other special effects such as distortion, ring modulation, phasing, wah wah, auto-panning, sampling, multi-tap echo, et-et-et-etcetera. There's a bazillion things you can do with these and combinations of effects that will require your own dedicated experimentation. I guess this is something like bungee jumping. It may be intimidating at first, but the results can be exhilarating. Or they may scare the begeebees out of you. (Imagine that, I've sunk to "bazillion" and "begeebees" in the same paragraph!)

9. SIGNAL CORPS

TO *BBE* OR NOT TO BBE . . .

Signal processing, if you'll remember, is a direct hookup that affects the whole signal. It can provide tremendous benefits, but you rarely get something for nothing (unless you're a politician). Anytime you process something, you can travel a little farther from its natural state. Maybe its natural state sounds like garbage so you have nothing to lose. But if it sounds decent, the trick is to get it through the system with as little mangling as possible. I've actually had recording clients come into the studio with one concern on their minds — how many graphic equalizers I had. "Sure, I do all my critical recording on a 1985 Tascam cassette Portastudio, and my 22 graphics make it sound like heaven!" Shoot me now.

Signal processing should never be a crutch for poor engineering or system design. Often it's a necessary element to help control levels for recording or to tune a room for optimum sound quality, and the advent of digital processing has eliminated much of our "mangling" concerns from analog circuitry and interfacing. But in many instances there are better and cheaper alternatives. Try a different mic, better speakers, improved mixer EQ technique, milk it for all it's worth before you patch in another device. When it *is* time, here are some of your choices...

AURAL ENHANCERS

Since I so cleverly used **BBE** in the header to make a point, I figured I should probably elaborate. This was a popular and economical sonic processor that could improve the clarity and dimension of a mix, a trait called "transparency" where the instruments and vocals stand out more clearly. With current digital technology, you can easily achieve this without a BBE, but it sure helped me through a lot of analog recording projects with some great results.

One aspect of the BBE's historical design is worth noting. It improved clarity by actually delaying the mid and low frequencies by a few milliseconds so the high frequencies would reach you first. This made them stand out more clearly due to different, yet imperceptible, timing. It's an interesting approach which also helped me understand how sound can work with speaker systems. You might detect this concept in some of my later discussions.

Another enhancement processor is the **aural exciter**. This one adds narrowband high harmonics for a sweet "breathy" high end, particularly for vocals. It uses harmonic distortion to achieve the effect, so I only used it on a few individual sources rather than on a collective mix. Like the BBE, you don't see these around much anymore except as standard studio furniture that can be exploited from time to time.

GRAPHIC EQ

A professional graphic equalizer breaks down the frequencies we studied into fifteen to thirty-one separate controls, allowing us to adjust them individually. Graphics are used primarily in live sound to correct for room acoustics and speaker-response deficiencies, and there are some easy clues as to when a system is well tuned: a CD should sound near studio perfect (allowing for room reverberation, of course) played through the system with its channel EQ set to flat, and so should a quality handheld vocal mic at about 6 inches. (If closer, the proximity effect of unidirectionals necessitates cutting back the low-channel EQ.)

Graphics include a level control for maintaining **unity gain**[2]. Once an EQ is set, hit the Bypass switch to see if the perceived level changes due to your EQ settings. If it does, adjust the level control so it's equal when you switch back and forth. This maintains proper levels through the system without loss or undue excess.

Since room and speaker anomalies are so varied, no one can tell you how to set a graphic. I *have* found that many rooms have problems around 100-160Hz and 315-400Hz, and horns may need control anywhere from 3kHz to 8kHz to smooth out peaks. Feedback frequencies also need to be addressed. If you want to get more accurate settings, read on.

Realtime Analyzer: This is a device designed to help you determine accurate response for your speakers. It's not a signal processor, but it needs mentioning here since it will help you set up a graphic equalizer. This unit has a broad LED or meter readout corresponding to all the frequencies of the graphic, a calibrated microphone for picking up all those frequencies, and a **pink noise** generator. Pink noise is all frequencies produced simultaneously and equally, as our ears perceive it, and sounds like what it implies — noise. Like a roomful of people all talking at the same time. Or maybe just your mother-in-law.

There's a tactic to using an analyzer. A good studio monitor has **flat**[21] (accurate) response as measured within a set distance. Add another speaker and you get more bass from "coupling." Move farther away and you lose high end from absorption in the air. Therefore, if I analyze combinations of speakers from too great a distance, I'll set the EQ for too much highs and not enough bass. (Think about it, or take my word for it.)

To balance things out, I find a spot to place the analyzer mic within the dispersion pattern of one speaker and no more than 50 feet back. Since any subwoofers in use are more omnidirectional, I just make sure I'm also in a decent spot for low end. With all EQ set to flat, pink noise is run into a channel and brought up through the speakers to an average expected performance volume. Now the pink noise, mixer, and amps constitute a flat signal. Any discrepancies read by the analyzer can, for all practical purposes, be attributed to the speakers or room, or both.

Mic sensitivity is set on the analyzer to a point where the meter levels are equally distributed on either side of the center line. Individual graphic EQ frequencies are then adjusted up or down opposite the analyzer, bringing the meters as close to a flat center line as possible. This corrects speaker response and compensates for major room resonances and reflections.

Afterwards, I'll analyze stage monitors at close range, then check for any consistent feedback problems by bringing up all the mics and fine-tuning graphics accordingly. As you can guess, an RTA can be a good investment and a great aid in developing a "Golden Ear." Current units start at around $400, and RTAs are sometimes included in the components of newer digital signal processors like the DBX Driverack series.

COMPRESSOR/LIMITER

You're running sound when suddenly the singer hits a high note that does a light show on your meters and turns your tweeters into confetti. You have three choices: shoot the singer, take up needlepoint, or add another set of helping hands — the compressor/limiter.

Compression gently controls level where **limiting** aggressively stops it. The **ratio** control determines which is occurring. A 1:1 ratio setting means for every 1dB of signal coming in, 1dB is getting out — no change, no compression. A 4:1 ratio means that for every 4dB of signal coming in, only 1dB is getting out — 75 percent compression, or one-fourth the peak we would have gotten otherwise. Anything greater than 10:1 is considered limiting. A **threshold** control sets the desired level at which the compressor will be activated, and our new hands are ready to start grabbing peaks. Other controls include input and output levels, **attack** and **release** to adjust reaction time and duration, and **knee** to soften the effect by having the compression start a little early and increase gradually. Check manuals for more details.

In the studio, I rarely use compression on sources other than vocals because I like to maintain natural dynamics, and many instrument peaks are due to resonant frequencies which I can control with EQ. Always use such processing sparingly to avoid squashing the sound. I wouldn't recommend using a compressor on an overall recording mix unless it's a quality tube or digital model, and only then at a mild 2:1 ratio. (Tubes and high-resolution digital are kinder and gentler.)

In live sound, I often use compression on most sources to control spontaneous peaks since digital mixers have provided the convenience. Limiting is used more for protection. It can be applied to main or monitor mixer outputs to avoid overdriving amplifiers and speakers. The threshold is set so that limiting starts just prior to amplifier clipping (overload). Where compression uses a more gradual "soft knee" response (representing a more rounded threshold curve), limiting can use a harder peak response (sometimes called "brick wall") to minimize any effect under the threshold. Many amps have some form of clip limiting built in. I recommend using it if it's available.

NOISE GATE[8]

A noise gate is an automatic on/off switch. Again you have a **threshold**, but this one is set at a minimum level where the gate should cut in. When used on a mic channel, a low or absent signal triggers the gate to cut off the mic so nothing else bleeds through.

A simple gate is generally found on most analog compressor/limiters. More complex dedicated units and digital processors will have adjustable **attack**, **hold**, **decay**, or **rate** controlling opening and closing duration, as well as **floor** or **range** to adjust the gate so that it never fully closes. A slow attack delays opening so that you could eliminate a problem at the start of a sound. A slow decay or rate will avoid noticeable cutoff of a gradually decaying sound like cymbals.

DIGITAL SIGNAL PROCESSORS

Now take every piece of equipment we've talked about in the last two chapters, add some basic mixer and metering functions, digitize it, put it all in a box with audio and computer connections, and you'll have the new generation of **DSP** (**D**igital **S**ignal **P**rocessing). Just like digital mixers, we now have almost unlimited flexibility with the components and configurations of total-system processing.

The first time I used a DSP unit, I had to laugh. I was sitting on my couch at home with a laptop, designing a sound system for a customer. I was dragging all types of audio gear onto the screen: meters, routing mixers, graphic equalizers, compressors, room delay, multi-effects, you name it. I felt like I was playing a video game!

By the time I was finished, I had a $20,000 processing system in a $5000 box. When I got to the facility, I downloaded my "video game" from the computer into the box, hooked up all the audio connections, fired up the system, and everything worked like a charm. I was sold! In fact, I ended up needing one more piece of gear in the system which would have cost another $1000 and taken at least a couple of days to get shipped in. I just dragged it onto the screen, connected a couple of "virtual cables," and I was done.

Peavey started this trend years back with their Media Matrix system and now most major manufacturers have some sort of DSP units available, geared primarily to live sound applications. Some lower-cost models (under $1000) have fixed configurations with fewer connections, maybe 2-in and 6-out. Bigger models will have more programming to design and control the elements as well as input/output options. (Yamaha's DME processors use the same I/O option cards as their digital mixers.)

These units will also allow you to store and recall different *scenes* like their mixer counterparts. One DSP unit can be controlling feeds to mains, monitors, audio and video recording, balconies, under balconies, halls, and offices. Then each memorized scene can be programmed to control which systems are on and how they're set for any given performance or function. Some can even be networked to other DSP units spread around a huge facility so they all act as one. Yes, the complexities of these units are best left to professionals, but they are great tools in everything from small churches to major arenas and concert halls.

Be aware that most of this digital processing is included in digital mixers, so you won't necessarily need both. I'm able to design most of my smaller systems with all signals going straight from mixer to amplifiers, and I suspect that future modular mixer designs may eliminate the need for external DSP altogether. For now, just leave room for one more piece in the equipment rack.

TUBE PROCESSORS

I might also mention the resurgence of **tube processing** in recent years. With the stark reality of digital recording, tubes are in greater demand for the warmth and "harmonic smoothing" they can offer. It's similar to the visual difference between video and film where film can have a softer, more pleasing appearance. Tube equipment like mic preamps, compressors, and

EQs cost more than solid-state and, if not a necessity, can at least offer an excellent variation from solid-state processing where desired.

In the same way, high-resolution digital mixers and processors can offer similar advantages due to the smoothness of the waveform and the absence of phase shift and distortion associated with analog equipment and integration. Think of this digital sound like HD (high-definition) video with the capacity for stunning clarity. It all depends on what you're looking for in your sound.

Another important processor is the **electronic crossover** (also included in digital signal processors). This requires an understanding of amplification and speaker components, so I choose to cover this in the speaker section. You got a problem with that?

10. POWER TOOLS

NO PAIN, NO GAIN

This is the macho section, dealing with devices of sheer brute force. . . heavy current draw. . . massive gain. . . shattered speakers. . . Tim Allen, eat your heart out! Amplifiers take our measly signals from the mixer and boost them enough to move speakers and, hopefully, our sense of good taste. Pro amps can provide power of 100 watts to 2,000 watts or more. Since these are the most powerful electronic devices we will be using, they possess the potential for doing the most damage. We want the right amp for our application and enough power for our needs without overloading anything along the way.

So Watt! So how much wattage is enough? Loose answers are based on several factors: "How many vocals/instruments do I have? Am I amplifying bass or drums? What are the capabilities of my speakers? How large is the area I need to cover?" (See, now I'm talking to myself.)

Let me just throw you some rough ideas in this area. Bare minimum I need is about 100 watts per channel stereo for near-field monitors in a small studio. In live sound, one watt per person room capacity is a reasonable starting point for main speakers, especially in churches and small performance venues. This should cover minimal needs at moderate volume, six to eight channels of vocals and light rhythm instruments (guitar, keyboard, kazoo, spoons, etc.). Increase total wattage proportionately to room and audience size. Stage monitors are fine with as little as 200 watts per channel.

For more powerful club and concert levels including contemporary worship in churches, 2 watts minimum per person (3 watts if sub-woofers are employed) should be available for mains along with speakers suited to the task. You can rarely have too much power, so our budgets will keep us within a practical range. The good news is that it can cost as little as $100 more to increase your power by 50 percent with current amp technology, so don't skimp unnecessarily on such a crucial need.

Sound Pressure: Now we need to understand how we hear these wattage differences. This can also be represented by *dBs* relative to the way we hear sound, and is called *SPL*[22] or *sound pressure level*. Where only about 10 percent of people can hear a 1dB change in level, around 50 percent of people can hear a 2dB change, and just about anybody can hear a 3dB change. Now the real kicker — an increase of 10dB sounds twice as loud, but it takes double the power to change the level only 3dB!

Consequently, if we have a 100-watt system, we need to get close to 800 watts to sound twice as loud! (Crazy, ain't it?) But that's if it depended on amps alone, which it doesn't. As with wattage, doubling our speakers also yields a 3dB increase. In that case, getting up to 400 watts with twice as many speakers should add a total of about 9dB. Keep this in mind as you assess your level needs. We'll cover more about SPL and speaker efficiency in chapter 11.

CHECKS & BALANCES

Amps take signals coming in and boost them tremendously, including any noise or *ground loops*[11]. So it's the same situation as the mixer input stage — *balanced*[10] inputs can become crucial. Again, they eliminate noise picked up along the length of the cable and allow you to lift grounds that cause hum. Unless all your equipment is situated close together, you shouldn't use an amp with unbalanced inputs. Otherwise, Murphy's Law dictates that you will most likely have problems. Wiring connections are the same as we discussed earlier.

Setting Level: As with mixers, the level controls on the amp should be set properly for the system. Optimum settings should drive the amp to maximum power when our mixer reaches the *unity gain*[2] "0dB" reading on its meters. At some point just over 0dB, we should see an overload indication on the amp. This way, we will always know how hard our system is working by our meter readings.

An easy way to set amp levels without breaking glassware is to unhook the speakers from the amp. (Don't do this with a tube amp!) With strong music or pink noise from an analyzer running through the mixer, bring up the master level until the meter hits +3dB (-3dB on digital mixers). Of course, all subsequent processors like equalizers and crossovers should be set for unity gain so you don't lose level along the way. Then bring up the amp level until you see its **overload**, or **clipping**, indicator just start to illuminate. That's your setting. Now you may cut off the test source, hook up your speakers, and repeat after me: "I will not push my meters over the limit. I know that is all the power I have. I do not want to blow my speakers and spend lots of money on repairs. Thank you Mr. White for saving my equipment. I'm sending $100 cash to show my appreciation."

If you find the system too loud for your needs with good meter readings, drop back the amp levels instead of the mixer to a level that is comfortable. This will give you a better signal-to-noise ratio. Make note of the previous higher amp settings for future reference in case you need to crank it up for a stronger program. If you can't quite get the amp to overload with the above procedure, you have my permission to raise graphic EQ or active crossover levels slightly to the point where it does. If it still won't, it's an indication you have a level problem or mismatched equipment. Ask a pro for help in pursuing the best solution.

Ohm, Sweet Ohm: Amplifier power is rated in relation to the amount of power draw by the speakers. It's listed in the specifications of the amp and determined by the **impedance** of the speaker load. You will see amp wattages based on 8Ω (*ohm*), 4Ω, and sometimes 2Ω loads, and they should correspond at least to what your speakers can handle if you expect to drive them to full power. (More speakers are damaged by too little power than they are by too much due to the stress in trying to reproduce a distorted amp signal.) There's also a rating called **bridged mono**, which we'll discuss shortly.

Most speakers are 8Ω and will indicate it near their connector plate. If you connect two 8Ω speakers to the same amp, the load halves and becomes 4Ω. You'll notice in amp specs that the wattage on a 4 load is typically one-third higher than 8Ω. So for the extra speaker we add, the amp provides more power. By the same token, two 4Ω loads make a 2Ω. However, the limit is usually 4Ω for most amps, below which they may eventually overheat and shut down. If our total speaker impedance load is too low, we will need more amps to accommodate them.

I will even go so far as to give you the only formula I intend to in this book:

$$Impedance = \frac{R1 \times R2}{R1 + R2}$$

R1 equals the impedance of one speaker, and R2 equals that of a second.

For example, if we have an 8Ω and a 4Ω speaker: $\frac{8 \times 4 = 32}{8 + 4 = 12} = 2.67Ω$

Obviously, this is too low for a minimum rating of 4Ω. So use this formula to make sure you're not overtaxing your amplifiers.

Amp Modes: Most professional amps are designed as a stereo, or dual, amplifier. They will operate as two amps in one package where each amp will handle its own load and can be used for individual purposes. Most have a special switch for different modes of operation. These include:

Stereo or Dual – each side of the amp receives its own source and functions independently of the other.

Parallel – the inputs of both amps are connected so they both receive a common source, though functioning independently in level settings and load.

Bridged Mono – both amps are electronically combined to form one BIG amp.

This is not meant as a designation for "non-stereo" applications!

This mode is for rare occasions when you have a speaker requiring more power than one channel of an amp can provide. If I wish to drive one 400-watt speaker with a 200-watt-per-channel dual amp, I can switch it to Bridged Mono and turn it into a single 400-watt amp. (And now for my next trick. . .) Only the first channel of the amp provides input and level in this mode. Be advised, however, that most amps are only rated to 8Ω in bridged mode, and there is a special method of hooking up the speakers. Please check your owner's manual for specifics.

70V Lines: In installations like churches or office buildings, you can end up with a mess of little speakers all over the place in ceilings, on walls, under balconies, wherever! This obviously causes a problem with total impedance, so the audio geeks of yesteryear came up with another idea. A 70V connection is designated on amplifiers that have it, and must be used with speakers equipped with 70V transformers. They are designed exclusively for this application.

These speakers have separate wire taps off their transformer for different wattages which we may choose for the speaker to draw. Since they are usually 8" speakers for covering small areas, the taps are typically 0.5 to 10 watts. In this situation, we are concerned with total wattage consumption instead of impedance. With a 100-watt amp, we can run up to 20 speakers wired at 5 watts each: 20 x 5 = 100. Or ten speakers at ten watts each. Simple math. Just do it.

CONNECTORS & CABLES[9]

Amp inputs are generally the same RCA phono, 1/4" phone, or XLR connections as found on mixers. On amp outputs and speaker inputs, however, connections available include 1/4" phone plugs, **Neutrik Speakon** connectors, or **5-way binding posts**. The *Speakon* are durable four to eight conductor plugs designed to accommodate professional enclosures including bi-amped, multi-wire connections. *Binding posts* are dual screw-down posts allowing the connection of bare wire or **dual banana plugs**. For each channel of a dual amp, there will be a red post for the *positive* (+) side and a black post for the *nega-tive* (−) side of the connection. In Bridged Mono mode, the red post of the first channel will be the *positive*, and the red post of the second channel will be the *negative*. Always double check your manual for proper connections.

Large gauge cable is used to carry the higher voltage output of amplifiers. Wires are run side by side like electrical cables and are not shielded like mic and line cables. There will be some conspicuous difference between the two wires for keeping positive and negative straight: copper/silver, white/black, ribbed/smooth, etc. Figuring for a single speaker from a 100- to 400-watt amp, I suggest a *minimum* of 16 gauge for cables up to 25 feet, 14 gauge up to 50 feet, and 12-gauge up to 100 feet. If in doubt, always go to the next larger gauge.

Going Through A Phase: I can't tell you how many times I have been to a performance or in a studio and heard speakers wired out of phase. Avoiding this just involves making sure the *positive* (+) connection of the speaker is hooked to the *positive* of the amp. *Double check yourself.* Otherwise, your sound will be screwy.

Your ears can also alert you with a quick test. With music playing, start in front of and facing one speaker, then gradually move towards the other speaker. When you get equidistant between the two, sound should appear centered. But if it suddenly sounds as if everything is split to both sides, they're out of phase. It's most likely the cable connections unless you had Goober rewire your cabinets.

If necessary, you can check to see if speaker cabinets are internally wired properly. With a cable plugged into the cabinet, quickly touch the positive and negative contacts of a 9V battery to the corresponding points on the other end of the cable. If the woofer jumps forward, every-thing's okay. If it jumps backward, connections are reversed. If it jumps sideways, seek counseling. If you can't see the woofer or don't know what it is, forget this test and proceed to chapter 10.

Proper polarity is important not only for the center imaging, but to avoid loss of overall response. Speakers out of phase are trying to cancel each other out. Once corrected, you'll notice better response from the whole system, and others will be amazed at your incredible abili-ty to detect the problem. A good way to make new friends and an interesting topic at parties. Pass the chips.

AMP EXTRAS

Amplifiers often incorporate other features that aid our efforts and eliminate the need and cost of extra components. Low-cut switches will allow us to roll sub-bass frequencies out of speakers that don't need it like stage monitors or ceiling speakers. Variable low-cut and crossover adjustments will control high and low frequencies for simpler full range + sub woofer systems so you can get by without an external crossover unit. Limiters will protect from overload, and some amps may include special speaker processing to improve speaker response or efficiency. Finally, newer commercial designs are providing computer connection for comprehensive display and network control of whole amp systems from the mix position.

There are also a few multi-amp designs with four to six amplifiers in one package. Though they are typically lower-power versions, they save cost and space for moderate needs such as monitors or 70V systems. Just be aware of some of these available options when you are shopping for an amplifier. They might save you a few hundred dollars.

11. PUMPING PAPER

If there is going to be a weak link in system design, it will likely be the speakers. This is because they have the most going against them. As with microphones, we are in a delicate position of transforming between electrical and acoustical energy. But microphones are single small elements picking up within a relatively short distance, minimizing our room for error. Speakers, however, use multiple large components required to blend together and cover large distances. Consequently, how well things are designed becomes vital.

S.P.L & R.U.Def

SPL[22] or *sound pressure level*, which we touched on in the amp section as a reference to how we hear wattage changes, is a measurement of actual intensity levels which our speakers can generate. It is based on a 0dB threshold of hearing with normal conversation at about 70dB, a strong gospel church service around 100dB, and some rock concerts capable of 120dB or more. Anything over 105dB can start getting uncomfortable depending on your tolerance, with 140dB considered the Official Threshold of Pain. Following are some of my examples of various levels. (For best effect, please read from bottom up):

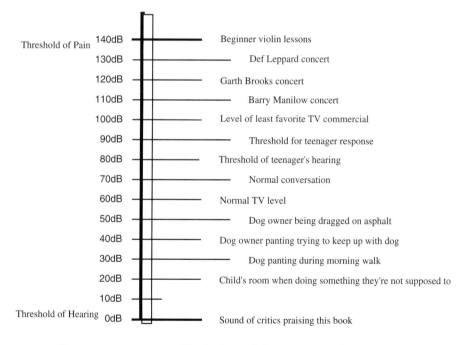

Threshold of Pain	140dB	Beginner violin lessons
	130dB	Def Leppard concert
	120dB	Garth Brooks concert
	110dB	Barry Manilow concert
	100dB	Level of least favorite TV commercial
	90dB	Threshold for teenager response
	80dB	Threshold of teenager's hearing
	70dB	Normal conversation
	60dB	Normal TV level
	50dB	Dog owner being dragged on asphalt
	40dB	Dog owner panting trying to keep up with dog
	30dB	Dog panting during morning walk
	20dB	Child's room when doing something they're not supposed to
	10dB	
Threshold of Hearing	0dB	Sound of critics praising this book

Our ears were actually designed for conversation. At speech levels, we have a peak in our hearing response around 3kHz where the definition is, while high- and low-end response is down considerably. In other words, we don't hear *flat*[21] at lower levels. This is the reason for a **loudness** or **contour** switch on many hi-fi systems. It's a boost for the low and high end to compensate for our low-level hearing response.

Yet an interesting thing happens when we start cranking up the volume. A little "compressor" in our brain starts grabbing the 3kHz spot while the other frequencies rise to catch up, until the response finally flattens out at around 90dB. That's why music sounds better when it's louder — our ears are hearing it right! (Sorry, Mom.)

For this reason, I'm usually going to be running music program closer to 90dB in the studio when I want to hear things accurately. But I want to keep dynamic concert sound within the 110dB range to avoid hearing damage. The exception is low end which I can drive to slightly higher "feel" levels, adding punch while avoiding excessive ear-damaging high-frequency levels. Be aware, though, that long durations of any high levels can affect your hearing.

STACKING UP

Back in the old days (that's Woodstock for many of us), the norm was big and bunches. We had separate boxes for tweeters, horns, mids, mid bass, bass, and Boones Farm. (Don't ask.) We had four-way and five-way crossovers. Hundreds of pounds of amps. And "narly" sound, dude! That's because all these mixed-bag components were doing their own thing and could rarely get it together. . . just like us.

With the vast improvements in speaker design and components, we now have systems that actually work together, take up less real estate, and sound good. We can get everything we need from **two-way** or **three-way speakers** and **subwoofers**, but how do we know which ones to get? Good hints are in the specifications of speakers, but they need to be looked at collectively. For instance, with near-field studio monitors, I'm mostly concerned with the **frequency response**. Larger PA speakers should also be scrutinized for **sensitivity** and **polar response**.

Sensitivity: Now you can use all that stuff you learned about *SPL*[22] where "doubling-wattageadds3dB" and "10dBistwicethevolume." Studio monitors, which are designed more for close-up use and moderate levels, will have sensitivity listings around 87dB. PA speakers will be around 97dB, a 10dB increase. This means that if you hook up a PA speaker in place of a studio monitor without changing the amp or level settings, it will sound at least twice as loud. Obviously, this is much better for high-level applications. In fact, just a 3dB difference in speaker efficiency can mean an increase comparable to doubling amp wattage. Remember?

Frequency Response: So if we see one PA speaker listed at 97dB and another at 100dB, buy the second one, right? Wrong! First, you have to look at the frequency-response graphs. They should appear as close to a *flat*[21] line as possible from 100Hz to over 15kHz. These may indicate that a louder speaker has a 4dB peak sticking up at 2kHz. So the speaker is louder due to a harsh peak, which can also

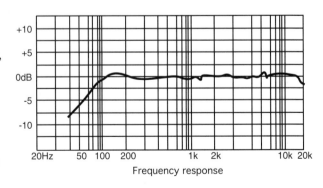

Frequency response

cause feedback. That isn't good. We don't want to sacrifice quality for volume. If that were the case, stadium horns would be perfect. (In fact, I believe that's what they use in hell for the audiophile section.)

Polar Response: PA speakers use horns to increase projection of high frequencies. Like a spotlight, horns *disperse*[23] these frequencies in a narrower pattern with higher velocity to throw farther in a large room. Unfortunately, the sound can get messed up from bouncing around in the horn chamber if the design doesn't perfectly complement the waveform created by the high-frequency driver on the back of the horn.

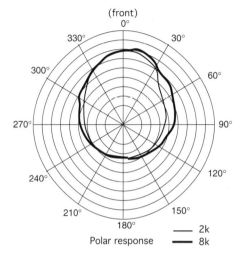

A polar reponse graph tells us how good that design is. A great horn will show almost perfectly matched oval lines from 2kHz to 16kHz. A bad one will have all kinds of weird shapes. This represents frequencies that peak out at certain positions around the cabinet and drop out at others, changing your sound and level considerably throughout the room. *Where the frequency-response curve tells how good the sound is directly in front of the cabinet, the polar response tells how good it is everywhere else!* All this taken into account, a good speaker design can become pretty obvious.

CROSSING OVER

You might remember I skipped over **crossovers** in the signal-processing section. Well, now it's time! These units help speakers do their job better and with less potential for damage. That's because they allow the various components to receive only the frequencies they're best suited for.

Full range speakers have two or three components: a **woofer** for low frequencies, a **tweeter** (or driver) for high frequencies, and sometimes an additional **mid-range** speaker dedicated to frequencies between the other two. Since the tweeter is very small compared to the woofer, it can't move enough to reproduce the lower frequencies and will be damaged by them. So the crossover filters out the low end going to the tweeter. Alternately, the woofer won't be damaged by high frequencies but does a sloppy job of reproducing the ones it can. So the crossover filters the highs from the low-frequency components. Similar concessions are made for a mid-range driver, with its range usually somewhere between 500Hz and 5kHz.

Most full-range speakers have a **passive crossover** (non-powered) built-in. This network takes the speaker signal coming in from the amplifier and does the filtering before it goes to the components in the cabinet. An **active crossover** is a powered unit which receives the line level signal from the mixer, then splits the frequencies *before the amps*. The individual amplifiers then provide their specific ranges directly to the appropriate components. Advantages of these powered units are that crossover points are more precise and can be adjusted, independent levels can be set for the various frequency ranges, and each amplifier can work a little easier doing a specific job.

Some amplifiers include a simple built-in active crossover which can be switched on and adjusted for the appropriate crossover frequency. Digital signal processors also incorporate active crossovers with comprehensive control and output routing, and some speaker manufacturers make dedicated crossover/processors configured to work with their own specified enclosures.

Except in larger applications, the quality of current internal passive crossovers is adequate for typical full range purposes. It's when using subwoofers that the active crossover becomes an essential addition as we'll learn in a moment.

STUDIO MONITORS

In the recording studio, we need an accurate set of speakers since every move we make is based on what we hear. Unlike many hi-fi speakers which are designed more for subjective and cosmetic appeal, studio monitors are designed with *flat response*[21] as a priority. The term implies smooth and accurate, not "bland" like a carbonated drink gone bad. With an accurate reference, we will be able to mix recordings well suited to all types of speakers.

Studio monitors are usually 2-way designs with woofers from 6–8 inches, or 3-way with woofers of 10–15 inches. They'll typically use 1" dome tweeters and 3–5" midrange drivers, though some larger models employ horns. Some popular manufacturers include JBL, KRK, Yamaha, Mackie, Bag End, and Genelec. Tannoy and Urei have offered models using coaxial speakers which employ a tweeter horn mounted in the middle of the woofer.

Active monitors have built-in amps and active crossover to maximize the performance of the speaker. Though high-end models are understandably pricey, most are more economical than buying separate components and they exhibit exceptional efficiency and sound quality. All the manufacturers above have active models available including compatible subwoofers so you can hear the lowest frequencies and know what's going on down there.

When choosing studio monitors, as with any speaker, the specs can tell us much of what we want to know but listening will tell us the most. All good speakers sound a little different and our preferences can be subjective, so pick one that appeals to you. And if you're not used to an accurate speaker, a good one will teach you a lot about how things *should* sound.

PA SPEAKERS

Full-range speakers typically use 10" to 15" woofers (though there are a few compact 8" and 5" designs) and horn drivers of 1–3 inches. Most are two-way since current high-end drivers do such a good job through the upper ranges. Some cabinets use cheaper **piezo** horns which should be avoided in all but minor applications. These elements are "beamy" and only reproduce above 6kHz, skipping right over the critical 2-5kHz presence range. True **compression driver** horns offer wide dispersion and response as well as better power handling.

Though I've used some dual 5"–8" models, I always use single woofer designs in full-size speakers and consider it errant to buy larger dual 15" full range with the idea that they will give you acceptable low-end performance. It is much better and similarly cost-effective to keep the full range compact and elevated for projection, and add **subwoofers** which are specifically made for efficient and powerful low end. It also makes 8" to 12" full range more practical since they're not required to handle bass, improving mid definition for vocals along with less size, weight, and cost.

There are quality, powered full-range PA enclosures with active crossover and amplifier built-in which I'm sure provide a portable convenience for some people. For me, I prefer running just one cable (the speaker line) to each cabinet and not having to provide both line signal and electrical power. And considering extra amplifier weight and any potential for electronic failure, I have more concerns if it's suspended in an installation. If a rack amp fails, I can simply switch to another one without the whole speaker going down. You can make up your own mind as to whether powered speakers are attractive in your application.

Waveguides & Line Array: These are two of the newer developments in PA horn design. The **circular waveguide** is being offered by a few companies like WorxAudio and ACE. Since all high frequencies emanate in a spherical pattern from a *circular* driver, it makes sense to have a circular horn to best retain that sonic integrity and avoid the transformation problems of changing a circle to a square. It's the closest I've heard to true high fidelity in conventional speakers that don't require dedicated processing, and I personally believe most designs other than line array should be using circular waveguide horns. In fact, one of the developers of what I consider the best designs that have evolved from the 1990s said, *"Waveguides are it! The industry just doesn't get it yet."*

Some advantages are that they tend to have a smoother and wider usable dispersion pattern without "beaminess," you can mount them in any rotated position with the same coverage, and the pattern is as high as it is wide for reaching first rows and balconies without supplemental speakers within their distance range. For some reason, the better designs are also less prone to comb filtering (the side-to-side phasing interaction due to high-end overlap between multiple speakers), likely because of their smoother dispersion.

Where waveguides are more economical and shine in a horizontal speaker array where the primary demand is width of coverage, **line arrays** offer much greater capability and control for depth of coverage. First introduced by L-Acoustics at the end of the last century, they have exploded on the market with variations by almost every major speaker manufacturer. The purpose here is multiple speakers that literally act as a vertical array of one. The high-frequency horn is designed as a vertical slot that serves to meld as a near-continuous line through each cabinet, resulting in the most seamless high-frequency coverage. The vertical design also helped to eliminate any perceived comb filtering since our ears are in a horizontal alignment.

Line-array enclosures have the tightest dispersion pattern, typically 120° horizontal by a mere 5°–15° vertical. As a result, you need enough enclosures to cover the degree of angle from front to rear seating. If you need increased projection, you can have two or more enclosures aligned parallel to work together for more distance. For instance, I could have two 5° designs on top pointing almost straight back to shoot 150 feet, four more in a progressively downward arc of 20° to cover the main floor up to 100 feet, and one 15° shorter throw on the bottom to catch the front rows. Brand-specific rigging hardware makes it easy to adjust the vertical angles of each speaker for optimum pattern control.

With their substantial width coverage, a single line array in a central cluster can often satisfy a room installation. If you need to cover more than a 120° width, however, you will need to fly additional line arrays or conventional fills on the sides. There are smaller units available like the Nexo GeoS series to accommodate a wide variety of more modest rooms and outdoor areas. These use a single 8" woofer design of 16 ohms (so you can run more off an amp), weigh less than 29 pounds each (so as not to tax structural support), and even include a horn adjustment that can change the width pattern from 120° to 80°, offering tighter coverage for multi-point systems or narrow venues.

Where some professional line-array enclosures run $5000 each, smaller models can run less than half that. Line-array manufacturers also normally offer a digital processor specially designed for optimum control, protection, and performance of the entire system. Though it all adds up to some expense, it's certainly worth it in the applications that demand such performance from the most unforgiving element of any sound package.

Subwoofers: Subwoofers are usually single or dual 15" or 18" enclosures designed to maximize low-end response. I normally prefer dual 15" indoors for their efficiency and naturally "tight" sound. (Larger 18" can't turn around as fast and tend to sound a bit overbearing indoors around the 80Hz range.) Subs should be dedicated to ranges below 125Hz depending on the system. I usually cross over subwoofers below 100Hz, and often below 70Hz in smaller rooms so I end up with more "feel" and less "mud" in close proximity to the cabinet. An active crossover either as a discreet component, built in to amplifiers or powered subs, or part of a digital signal processor will provide this range to the subwoofer and can filter low frequencies out of our full range so they can work easier and cleaner, too. The full range can be elevated for better coverage and the subwoofers left on the floor for maximum efficiency.

The reason for this efficiency is the omnidirectionality of low end. It uses planes, like a floor or wall, as an acoustic "amplifier" to increase level in the room. In fact, I can get at least 6dB more bass and better distribution throughout most rooms by placing the sub on the floor and pointing it towards a wall, within a few inches to a foot. I equip some venues with two to four small suspended speakers, and one or two subs placed to the rear or side of the stage area this way. Unless you're standing near them, you don't know where the low end is coming from! Most people just think the full-range speakers sound that incredible. (This is the trick Bose has effectively used with their little cube+subwoofer home system.)

Spot Check: With any full-range speaker, particular attention should be given to the horn *dispersion*[23]. Just as with mic pickup, we can direct speakers like spotlights to cover the necessary areas. Plus, we want our stage mics to be out of the horn pattern to minimize feedback. Floor monitors (compact wedge versions of our full range) are designed to cover your stage needs.

Put your wrists together and angle your palms out to form a right angle. Then point out towards the room and you can approximate the area a typical 90° horn should cover. (You see, it's common sense but even "professional" installers still mess up on coverage angles.) Speakers with 60–75° horns can throw more evenly over a longer distance, so use these when you need to project over 50 feet. Just narrow the palm angle slightly to spot-check.

Another concern is if you have to hit a balcony. You can adjust your palm angle sideways to get some idea if the typical 45° vertical pattern of a square horn will catch it. Circular wave-guide horns make this easier since their pattern is 60–75° all around, and line arrays allow you to add and adjust speakers for more specific coverage. If a conventional speaker doesn't project high or far enough, you will need to add delayed speakers in front of the balcony areas or bite the bullet and invest in a line array system.

Stage Monitors: Monitor enclosures are slanted floor versions of our 2-way full range using 8" to 15" woofers. There are also smaller designs like the Galaxy Hot Spot with one or two 5" speakers. These are especially useful for providing good mid/high definition to one or two performers within a small area, and minimizing excessive low end from the stage caused by larger, "bassier" floor monitors.

In-Ear Monitors: Though it strays slightly from our emphasis on speakers for the moment, it's important to address the development of **in-ear monitoring (IEM)** in both multi-channel and wireless versions. IEM can eliminate the amplifiers, cabling, stage monitor levels, and potential feedback of monitor speakers while offering a better mix that can potentially follow your artist to the ends of the earth (if you can transmit that far). Wireless models use an audio transmitter and a receiver pack that operates in stereo on UHF frequencies, they utilize small earphones that are inconspicuous and can block outside sound, and they have dropped to under $1000 from companies like Shure and Sennheiser. These systems also have a "dual-mono" mode which allows you to switch the stereo feed to two mono feeds from a single transmitter which can then be individually selected on multiple receiver packs. At this writing, Galaxy Audio has released a more basic IEM wireless system for under $500.

Companies like HearTechnologies and Aviom offer affordable multichannel, wired in-ear systems with significant advantages when freedom of movement is minimal. These systems respectively handle a combination of eight or sixteen feeds from auxes, insert sends, or direct outs to a multichannel hub. The hub then sends all signals through ethernet cables to individual remotes equipped with separate level controls for each feed, and everyone controls their own personal monitor mix. Though the larger Aviom system is around twice the cost of the Hearback, it has many advantages including daisy chaining, tone control, stereo panning, mix memories, and a cost-saving hub designed as an option card for installation in Yamaha digital mixers.

Monitoring options include hooking the earphone output of the remote into a wireless IEM transmitter so you'll have both mix control and untethered movement. I've also patched it to a powered monitor or, via a floor-box connection, to an existing amp rack powering standard floor wedges. (With any IEM, be aware of the possibility of hearing damage if users aren't smart about adjusting their earphone levels, and hygiene concerns if earpieces are used by different people.)

DELAY LINES[18]

If you have seating out of the throw or line of sight of the main speakers such as under a balcony, you will need speakers dedicated to the area. Whether extra full-range or small ceiling speakers, they will need to be on a high-quality digital room-delay processor inserted before their amplifier to compensate for distances of 40 feet or more between them and the main speakers. Otherwise, you will have a noticeable echo between the two that blurs the sound. (Digital mixers normally have built-in delay on their outputs so no external unit is needed.)

The delay time should be set at just under 1 millisecond per foot of distance between the main and delayed speakers, or you may tune it by ear with a well-defined rhythm source such as drums on a soundtrack. While listening in the delayed area, have someone at the processor increase the delay time setting until you hear

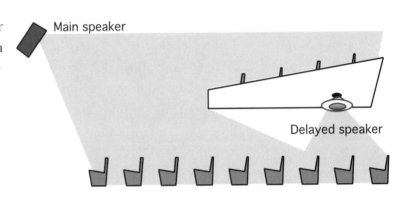

Main speaker

Delayed speaker

the echo disappear between the main and delayed speakers, and the rhythm hits occur simultaneously. From that point, increase the delay time another 5ms and the delayed speakers will almost seem to disappear. This is a result of the ***Haas effect***[19], as mentioned in chapter 8. When the room delay is set just a few milliseconds longer than needed, the ear is fooled into thinking the sound is coming from the original source. It's important, however, that the delayed system level and EQ be set to only supplement the mains as needed. Most of the time, subtle mid/high definition is all that's required. Low and low-mid frequencies from the main speakers will usually reach or reflect into the delayed areas, adding body and supporting the **point-source reference** (sound perceived to emanate from the direction of the source).

If you have a real deep underbalcony, you may need to compromise the delay setting for ceiling speakers at different depths or incorporate another delayed region. Another choice would be to suspend small, quality two-way speakers with horns flush to the underbalcony ceiling near the front edge and facing back. A dual 5" or other compact waveguide design with a wide-dispersion horn will excel here, and would carry at least 30 feet if you have a drywall ceiling (or similarly reflective drop-ceiling tiles), and point the speaker straight back with no downward angle. This avoids blasting people near the front and helps reflect sound off the ceiling to the rear seats.

12. FOR THE RECORD

RECORDING

Economical digital multitrack recorders preceded digital mixers by a few years in the early nineties, and opened up a whole new world for the average musician and garage studio. Semipro tape recorders had served us well, but they were rendered obsolete by the quality, convenience, and expandability of these new systems. Initially, digital had its own set of problems to overcome, but current products truly offer a level of performance previously unimagined in their price range. And just like digital mixers, they give us production potential that is still being advanced today.

I suspect we are on the verge of newer technologies that will provide increased and dependable storage for audio as well as video recording. Many of the older formats discussed below are essentially obsolete, replaced by hard disk and promising formats like DVD. But at this point, hard disks are not a cheap removable format, and DVD is highly prone to damage since it is not protected by a shell like video tapes or MD and MO discs. Hopefully, we'll soon see a cheap, real-time-writable (that means you can record straight to it), high-density removable format that won't scratch that all recorders (and high-definition video) can use. And it will have to be bigger than a jump drive so you can stack it and put a label on the darn thing!

For legacy's sake, I'm going to cover all the digital formats and features from the start of the 1990s explosion. Some of you may still have some older recorders in your arsenal or see them showing up as good buys on eBay. If nothing else, it's an interesting study on the ingenuity of manufacturers to satisfy the needs and creative potential of the masses.

RECORDERS

Professional 24-track analog recorders using 2" reel tape are still found in many studios. Like tube technology, analog has unique musical characteristics based on the subtle ways it captures sound rather than its total perfection in reproducing it. But $25,000+ for a good machine plus 2" tape costs at 30 IPS (over $100 for 15 minutes!) was prohibitive for the average musician's budget.

The new digital recorders and **workstations** (recorder/mixer combinations) offer high-quality reproduction at much lower cost, and unprecedented capabilities only possible with digital. Though there's been a lot of argument over analog versus digital through the years, current technology, its track record, and the market has settled the matter. Personally I welcome all that digital has to offer and I've found ways to duplicate desired analog characteristics as needed using creative micing, EQ, compression, and/or tube processing.

MDM Recorders: **M**odular **D**igital **M**ultitracks introduced by Alesis and Tascam used high-resolution **SVHS** or **Hi8** video tape to record digital audio. Adapting a digital format to economical and readily available video transports brought costs down to those previously associated with semipro tape machines, and advantages over those were numerous:

1. There was no inherent tape noise to contend with.
2. There was no need for sound-degrading noise reduction.
3. Spot editing (punch in/punch out) was totally seamless.
4. You could bounce or transfer tracks with no loss of quality.
5. Audio reproduction was consistent from machine to machine.
6. Synchronizing of multiple machines was simple and much more accurate.
7. Complex software-based functions were possible such as digital routing, track delay, and programmed recording.

They function pretty much like a normal tape recorder, just with all the added capabilities. The only maintenance is periodic cleaning which is the same as for a video deck. Head life is estimated at 2000 hours or more. Alesis ADAT recorders will even tell you how many actual hours of use are on the head.

A unique feature of MDMs was their inherent ability to synchronize together for more tracks. Big reel machines required expensive servomotors and synchronizers to lock together. MDMs needed only to loosely sync the motors; digital buffers made sure the audio was output precisely to time code clocked at 48,000 times a second. It also made it much more cost-effective to manufacture a single 8-track model rather than divide production between 16- and 24-track models, too. Now you could just buy as many 8-tracks as you needed and lock them up. They could be synced to video or MIDI sequencing gear as well using available interfaces.

MDMs can be set to 48k or 44.1k sampling rate, the latter being the CD manufacturing standard. Recording time per tape varied from 40 to 100 minutes depending on the machine. These unique inventions also demanded innovation in transferring eight digital tracks through a cable, so two new formats were devised: *ADAT* optical by Alesis and *TDIF* multipin by Tascam. These have become multichannel interfacing standards in current digital systems including recording, mixing, processing, and I/O option accessories.

Hard Disk Recorders: These multitrack units offer all the advantages of MDM tape systems plus more recording time and random-access location and editing capabilities. Like CDs, you can go to any point on your recording instantaneously, as well as copy, delete, and move things around. This is possible since information is being read off a computer hard disk as opposed to a linear piece of tape.

Many systems are totally software based and require a compatible computer, but there are a few self-contained hardware systems from sixteen to twenty-four tracks by Alesis, Mackie, Fostex, and Otari. Many offer **waveform editing** as an integral or optional feature. This allows you to actually see the waveform on a screen where you can do creative (or wacky) things to it: edit out noises or breath sounds, alter whole words, duplicate parts, etc. Loads of fun for the whole family!

You can also create different versions of a recording. Re-recording various sections to other locations is the copy method. But another feature called the **playlist** allows you to designate different sections of a recording and simply program them to be played back in different arrangements without copying and using up more disk memory.

Hard disk recorders have become very economical, driving the older digital tape units to extinction, though available memory is at the mercy of present but rapidly progressing technology. Internal hard disk size in older units can range from a mere 540 megabytes, which holds about 100 minutes of 16-bit audio, to 40 gigabytes (40,000 megabytes) or more in newer units for more than 100 hours worth! This is total time which you'll have to divide by the number of recorded tracks and reduce for higher 24-bit resolution recording. Hookups for external SCSI drives can offer even more memory for recording and archiving, and CDR or CDRW can be a convenient removable medium for storing up to 700MB of data in addition to being an audio mastering format. There are also emerging "data compression" schemes and formats that stand ready to increase recording time and capabilities.

MiniDisc (or MD) Recorders: The Sony MiniDisc format was successfully exploited in the multitrack market for a time with 4-track and 8-track units by Sony, Yamaha, and Tascam. The MDs offered many of the advantages of hard disk but on a cost-effective and removable MD Data Disc in a protective "floppy disk" style shell which holds about 140 minutes total time, eliminating the need for off-loading data. They also proved useful for live production sound tracks in theatre with instant cueing like CDs, song titling, and extra tracks for adding voice-overs, sound effects, and overlapping song transitions. MDs utilize a proprietary data-compression scheme, so they were never considered a "full-quality" professional format.

Magneto-Optical (MO) Recorders: MO was a promising format that got lost in the transitional shuffle of new technologies, falling somewhere between a recordable CD and a MiniDisc: random access, re-recordable, housed in a casing (like MD), available in 3.5" and 5" versions, and recording *non-compressed* audio. Though first introduced by Akai with their earlier DD1000 2-track, it surfaced again in short-lived modular 8-track models by HHB and Yamaha. Everything you always wanted in a MiniDisc… and more. I wouldn't mind seeing an economical version of the MO media revived as a dual-sided DVD-Pro format protected by a shell. How about it all you media manufacturers?

DAT Recorders: **D**igital **A**udio **T**ape recorders were the first affordable digital format available. Originally designed as a consumer product, it was soon clear that consumers wouldn't take the bait and DATs ended up being adopted by the pro audio industry as a standard format for cassette and CD manufacture. They record stereo digital audio on special DAT tapes sharing a single data track, and are not capable of punch in/out editing or recording separate tracks. Though subject to the normal wear of tape and mechanics, they established their reliability over the years. There were even a few portable "Walkman-type" models which I loved to sneak into concerts or presidential cabinet meetings. (I still have my old Casio DA-R100 portable that's as small as a digital camera.)

DATs will record up to 120 minutes of audio at 48kHz or 44.1kHz standards, and some have the capability of 32kHz "nonlinear" long-play recording for up to 4 hours. This limits frequency response to about 15kHz, so I only used it for noncritical programs, lectures, and saving my old record albums, scratches and all.

CD Recorders (CDR): I'm sure you're acquainted with CDs, but it's really only in recent years that we've had affordable, recordable, portable, wish-we'd-had-'em-before-dable CD recorders. Three formats have been available: the pro-format CDR which records audio or data on standard blank CDs and, for consumer recorders, *digital audio* CDR that records only audio and CDRW that records on rewritable CDs. The reason for the latter two was to give record companies a little dividend from sales due to obvious home copying, plus protection from mass-population pirating. Consumer CDR(W) recorders are cheaper, but they incorporate "copy prohibit" in the format to prevent direct digital copies from being made.

When we finally had the luxury of mix automation with some digital mixers, I switched to CD for my mastering medium. Before affordable automation, we were destined to make numerous attempts at the final mix, trying to get all those knob and fader moves just right. Since write-once pro CDRs could not be re-recorded after a mistake, re-recordable DAT or hard-drive mastering was our logical choice. But now automation could be our master! All settings and moves are recorded in the mix software so you just start the CDR, hit the *automix* button, and a perfect mix is transferred while you sit back and enjoy your prune juice. Some multitrack workstations like the Yamaha AW4416 had it all: the digital mixer with mix automation, an extra stereo track for mixdown, and a built-in CDR for mastering and data storage.

MP3: I can't conclude digital recording without mentioning iPods and mp3. Years ago there was portable radio that you could carry around, and then cassette, and then CD Walkman, but they all lacked selection, quality, or quantity. Now you can live in your own universe devoid of the world around you with thousands of songs streaming from your pocket into your earbuds. (Is that a good thing?) This was made possible by the *mp3* recording format that condensed stereo audio down to one-tenth the size of noncompressed CD audio. Though not a pro-format because of the compression scheme (which does affect the sound), it certainly is the best combination of quality and quantity to come along, and has made it possible to have internet access to an unlimited catalog of songs. Just don't let it render you a non-productive member of society, or mislead you into plundering the investment and hard work of the music makers.

It won't be long for this section to make the Smithsonian with all the continuous advances in digital audio. Eventually, all digital equipment should be able to fully integrate and communicate. The near future should spawn more in recordable multitrack media, googlabytes of random-access memory (RAM), and maybe even Dilithium-crystal recording with warp drives! Stardate... sooner than you think.

Cassette Multitracks: For the beginners or cost conscious, there may still be a few 4-track cassette recorders on the store shelves. They use standard high-bias cassettes, and have a basic mixer with adequate quality and EQ control. They're easy to use and provide a useful experience in recording and production techniques.

Regular stereo cassette players are 4-track formats, but they only record stereo tracks (left and right) on one edge of the tape. When you flip the cassette over, it records stereo tracks on the other edge in the opposite direction. Cassette multitracks record all four tracks simultaneously (or one track at a time) in the same direction covering the whole tape, so you don't flip the cassette over. For better quality, most units run at twice the speed of normal stereo decks. Think of it as more tape going by providing more "memory" space for storing information.

When complete, your multitrack recording can be mixed to a regular stereo recording deck. Of course, you can't play a 4-track cassette recording on a regular cassette player for several reasons: it only plays two of the tracks at once, the other two are going in the wrong direction, high-speed recording will result in very slow playback, and noise reduction may not be compatible (like DBX or Dolby S). But who am I to say. . . you may like your music this way!

A common procedure in multitracking with such 4-tracks is **bouncing** or **ping-ponging**. This involves recording three tracks, then mixing and re-recording them together to track 4. Once you get the bounce the way you like it, you can erase those first three tracks and record three new things on them. Or record two and bounce those to track 3. You can end up with seven or more total tracks, but you lose considerable quality along the way. (Remember, this is analog.) When you're ready for better quality, you simply spend a little more and go digital.

VIRTUAL TRACKING

If you have keyboards, sound modules, drum machines, and MIDI sequencing capability, you already have a "digital recording" system. Though it only plays back MIDI parts, you can synchronize it to a digital multitrack and have both play together in perfect time. This is called **MIDI sync**, and we even used to do it with tape multitracks using a tape-to-sync interface like the J.L. Cooper PPS-2. With most digital systems, MIDI sync can work in both directions (either sequencer as master and multitrack as slave or vice versa), and it will tell the slave when and where to start and how fast to go.

Suddenly, all your sequenced outputs become additional live tracks playing along with your multitrack system. You won't need to record these parts and use up tracks, you can make quick changes at any time by simply editing your sequences, and any keyboards or modules you add become more MIDI tracks. All you need is additional mixer channels to handle the extra outputs which, it so happens, are available or expandable on most digital mixers and workstations.

13. AUDIO BY DESIGN

It's time I confessed something, and it will probably blow any semblance of credibility and wisdom I've attempted to build to this point. . . "I bought a used 1987 Hyundai." There, I said it, but let me explain. I got a good deal. (Obviously.) It looked to be in good shape. (Okay, I wasn't wearing my glasses.) Everything seemed to be put together well. (So now I'm an automotive engineer!) And the thing was an endless deluge of disenchantment.

Somehow I missed the point. While ignorantly considering its apparent outward condition, I overlooked a more important concept. . . something having to do with *MOTION*. The same thing can happen with audio. You need some idea of what you're trying to accomplish, or you're going nowhere. All the fancy tools are worthless without realistic goals. I hope to start you on a basic blueprint in this section.

(Note: To be fair, Hyundai has improved since the 1980s and I now proudly drive a Sonata.)

> *You need some idea of what you're trying to achieve, or you're going nowhere.*

RECORDING

The studio is the most controlled and critical audio environment, making it a great spot to sharpen your skills, train your ears, and experiment with ideas. Unlike live sound situations, there are few background noises and room reflections to mask the audio details you need to hear, you have the luxury of being able to do "one more take" until you get it the way you want it, and you have an excellent reference on which to base your results — national-quality recordings. You can listen to them side by side with your projects to make immediate comparisons and corrections.

If things sound too good to be true, they are. There is an inherent problem with recording that the uninitiated fail to consider. In a live performance, you have sound arriving at your ears from a multitude of sources and directions. Each ear receives these soundwaves with all kinds of complex location information to help separate and clarify the different components and direction of the sounds.

In *stereo* production, all this needs to be duplicated by two speakers, two positions. A lot of critical information is missing, limiting the ear's ability to distinguish the sources and their placement clearly. So we must compensate somehow to help simulate (and stimulate) the "transparency" of the natural environment. This is done with what I call **"The Five P's of Production."**

Frequency Pockets: Vocals, guitars, keyboards, bass, horns, drums. . . all this conglomeration gets jammed through speakers and suddenly it's like a small room crowded with people. They're stepping on each others toes, and it's hard to see who's who. If we can dress them all in different colored clothes and spread them out more, maybe we can improve the situation.

In mixing, the different instruments can quickly start muddling together, especially in the lower frequencies where bass starts piling up. *My first fix is to roll bass EQ out of non-bass sources.* Voices, guitars, horns, most keyboard parts, etc. don't need much, if any, low end below 100Hz. What *is* there usually consists of boominess or muddiness that will get in the way of bass and kick drum, and destroy clarifying contrast between low- and high-end sounds. So take it out on appropriate channels to the point where the sound clears up, but before it gets too thin.

Next, we'll start identifying and dedicating the frequency ranges where our individual instruments best fit. For example, kick drum "feel" is concentrated around 50-70Hz, so maybe I'll EQ the bass guitar for the 70–200Hz range with definition up to 1kHz. Keyboards can provide warmth and body through the 200–600Hz range with highs up to 6kHz, so I'll EQ the lead guitar to stand out in the 500–800Hz range with some bite at 2kHz. I could also take frequencies above 8kHz out of both to make room for the high-end "brilliance" of vocals and cymbals. Sax will fit nicely in the 700Hz-5kHz spot and vocals, with their slightly higher levels, should predominate from 400Hz to 12kHz. Cymbals and some percussion will top everything off with sweet highs up over 10kHz.

Though these are only examples and other frequencies are present in all these instruments, giving each its own special "pocket" makes them more discernable and evens out levels throughout the frequency spectrum. In fact, with a **realtime analyzer** hooked up, you can get visual indication where each instrument is in the mix, and experiment with getting a smoother response on your recordings. As I discussed in the section on equalizers, much of this is accomplished by cutting back nonessential frequencies rather than overboosting the desired ones. This takes a bit of work, and lends itself to the next important aspect of mixing.

Priorities (also known as Commitment): No room for "wishy-washy" Charlie Browns here. When I use creative EQ to improve overall balance and separation, I also commit to something definite which listeners will be able to identify and relate to. And I can choose to be conspicuously different or even radical in this endeavor, attracting attention to the music and its components.

Such easily recognizable aspects of a song, in composition *or* production, are called **hooks**. The more good ones you have, the more likely the song will be noticed. The same concept applies to instrument balance. Everybody can't be the "star." *Pick the strongest and most dominant themes and commit those out front.* Mix the rest comfortably in the background to create a good foundation of support. If there isn't a dominant memorable theme, create one! Don't just jam up a bunch of weak ideas. The song is only as strong as its weakest link.

Sometimes it may seem hard to keep priorities like vocals from getting enveloped by other sounds. The trick is using pockets along with keeping the denser instruments lower in the mix. You may need to EQ down the over 2kHz range on keyboards or distortion guitar to make more room for vocal presence. I prefer to get more power out of my mixes by kicking the drums strong since they offer a lot of open spaces for the vocals to come through. Then my rhythm instruments will collectively equal the level of the drums. Bass is adjusted to add fullness to the overall mix. Finally, I'll ride the leads and instrumental hooks, bringing them up and down to fill in gaps between vocal parts.

Be aware of the tendency for vocals to collectively exceed a desired overall level. When harmony parts come in, don't bring them up to the lead. Rather, have them set at least 3dB lower and blend the lead back into them, maintaining a more consistent overall level and avoiding peaks.

Panning[15]: We'll use the stereo channel pans to move things left and right in the mix and create a 2-dimensional image. I designate settings as clock positions: 9:00, 2:00, 12:00, etc. Except for actual stereo tracks such as keyboards, effects, or stereo mic pairs, I usually don't pan sources full left and right. It can sound like one ear is stopped up if you're wearing headphones.

I also give a lot of consideration to panning sources with similar characteristics to opposite sides for better balance and separation. If the hi hat is panned right, the high-end-percussive acoustic guitar is left. If sax is left, lead guitar is right. Sopranos right, altos left, and so on. Pan everything a little differently to maximize separation, and make sure your left/right metering maintains an even balance. This usually means that the strong low-end sources such as bass and kick drum should remain centered.

Perspective: Mic technique can be a crucial aspect in creating a 3-dimensional perspective. **Stereo micing**[5] is one of the most effective because it captures natural room characteristics recognizable to our ears. The better the room ambience, the better the effect. And using this technique for recording background vocalists or other multiple sources all together provides the imaging of each element being in a unique position in the mix.

When close micing a single source, you could record another mic strategically placed back in the room to pick up the ambience. Pan the two to opposite sides in the mix and you get a nice natural effect.

Try switching *phase reverse*[14] on some channels at mixdown if you have it available. This is a feature on high-end and digital consoles and is used to switch the polarity of the source signal. I've used it on background vocals, cymbals, and high-end percussion with some slight but noticeable changes in front-to-back perspective. *Do not* use this on one side of a stereo source since it will cause phase cancellation.

Of course, there have been a few black boxes offering simulated 3-D and surround alternatives, but we must assume that most won't sound compatible on other systems short of going to a full-digital surround standard. Used discreetly, some like the earlier Hughes Retriever gave me successful results on specific stereo tracks such as drum overheads, background vocals, and stereo effects, pulling them out in front of the two-speaker plane as much as a foot. If you get a chance, you might experiment with the potential of these devices if there are any available. You may come up with your own sound and special effects.

Processing: Digital effects are the second stage of developing our 3-dimensional image, with *reverbs*[20] being the most common addition. These will simulate the space of a variety of rooms. An easy way to make a source sound more distant is to roll off EQ above 5kHz and add more reverb, simulating the added ambience and loss of high end over distance. Another technique I use is recording a lead vocal twice, then mixing the first dry and the second as *full* reverb (no original signal) subtly blended in. The slight timing differences between the two make for a deeper, more dimensional sound. You can also set reverb **pre-delay** for an intended room depth, say a rough setting of 60ms for 60 feet. (Some effects let you switch delay increments from milliseconds to feet.)

Along with some additional notes in the Cause & Effect chapter, there are endless possibilities that you'll just have to jump in and explore.

LIVE RECORDING

I've had a few people recently who wanted to have the capability of multitrack recording and live mixing simultaneously. The problem with using direct and group outs from a live console to the multitrack is that any channel EQ or level adjustments for the house mix are going to be printed to tracks, and they may not be constructive. A digital console offers more flexibility here, with digital outputs and a lot of routing options including pre-fader direct outs.

A useful approach for portable recording with various analog mixers is to invest in some 8-channel rackmount mic preamps, 3 of which can feed 24 tracks. Just send mic lines through these to the multitrack, set levels with enough headroom at the sound check, and let it roll. Either a split snake or the multitrack outputs (in *Input* mode) can be fed to the live console, and a totally independent mix for the house can be achieved. Another option is using the mixer channel inserts as pre-fader sends to the recorder (discussed on page 34) if distance is short since lines will be unbalanced. Unlike direct outs, inserts are normally pre-EQ so that EQ changes on the house mix will not affect recording.

As I briefly mentioned in the Microphone section, orchestral recording could be accomplished with just a quality ***stereo pair***[5] in the hall. With multitrack capability, however, we have the luxury of section micing to give us more mix control. One concern of mine is the potential distance and delay between the hall mics and any section mics used. Solutions are minimizing the distance or using high-resolution channel ***delay***[18] available in digital mixers. In the mixdown, we can delay those individual section tracks to match the distance of the hall mics, achieving a perfect combination of natural stereo sound along with intimate instrumental detail and balance. In other words, you can have your cake and eat it too!

If you're just doing a stereo feed straight off the main mixer outputs, you may find your record mix balance a little off. The live mix is a calculated blend of system *and* ambient sound, with the softer elements like vocals or violins reinforced more, the louder elements like brass or percussion reinforced less. By contrast, the recorder *only* sees the system signal which may result in soft stuff blasting and loud stuff in the background. The smaller the room, the more pronounced the inconsistency. It's best to use dual or stereo post-fader aux outputs, or a split feed to another mixer so compensated level adjustments can be made to the individual channels, creating a custom balance of your mix for stereo recording.

Final Notes: Here are some last minute tips before you fall into the piteous pit of perpetual production pursuits:

- Always get good levels to tracks, even with digital. It improves digital resolution and will aid console signal-to-noise.
- Don't overdue low end! If you want to hear a 9dB boost below 60Hz, crank up subwoofers. Don't try to cram it on tracks and eat up your dynamic range.
- Use compressors conservatively for the least side effects. If you wish to mildly limit the whole mix, use a quality tube or digital processor for best results.
- When recording a drum set, get at least one minute of just toms and cymbals at the head of the tracks. This will make it easier to get mixdown settings on them since they are usually sparse in the music itself.
- If lacking in effects units, print the less ambient ones to tracks like echoes, pitch shift, etc. Save dimensional reverbs and delays for the final mix.
- Always check your final mixes at low volume levels where your ears become a "mid-reference." Listen for overall balance, making sure the instruments don't get wimpy in relation to the vocals. Everything should still be distinct.
- Always commend any producer on how lovely (he/she) looks today.

LIVE SOUND

I chose to cover recording first, because most of its aspects will carry over beautifully here. Obviously, studio quality sound would be optimum, but it is difficult to achieve due to the nature of this "uncontrolled" environment. (This implies that you will be forced to adapt to the characteristics of the many rooms you may be working in.) Fortunately, the energy and visual stimulation of a live performance help mask many of the subtler flaws and add to the overall impact of the sound, but we'll still have to deal with room acoustics, stage volume, background noise, speaker tuning, level and coverage requirements, and hecklers demanding Lynyrd Skynyrd and Aerosmith. And that's just in a Christian concert!

High wattage and levels are major concerns here. The whole idea of a live performance is often to be conspicuous and dynamic, and this must be maintained over any competing levels from enthusiastic crowd response. Unfortunately, many groups are trying to squeeze too much out of an inadequate system. If you have quality speakers well matched to amplification, system gain set up properly, mixer meters hitting at **unity gain**[2] and you still don't have enough level, you need more speakers and amps. Simple. *Save up!*

In live sound, I find myself pushing the 60Hz low end of the system a little hotter to increase "punch" and perceived level without resorting to excessive high frequencies that can damage hearing. Depending on the room, I may also add a touch more above 10kHz to carry brilliance, especially in vocals. I'll make up headroom with **subsonic filtering**, taking out frequencies below 40Hz on my master EQ. This tightens up the bottom end and saves wattage.

When you're hooking up your system, also be aware of the current draw of all your amplifiers. It is usually listed on the back of the amps by the AC cord or fuse, and is listed in amperes such as "12A." If they only show *electrical* wattage (not the speaker wattage), use the formula WATTAGE ÷ 110 = AMPERES. (The 110 is the voltage off the wall.) The reason you need to know this is so you don't overload the electrical wall circuits, most of which are only 15–20A each. Unless you're equipped for high-power taps, request and use 20A circuits if available, and divide up amps to different circuits if necessary. Be aware of the potential for ground loops if you do. The good news is that some newer amps like the Yamaha EEE designs draw as little as half the current of previous models. You should check these specs if you anticipate power limitations.

The *Few Less* P's of *Performance* Production: Why less? Because we aren't concerned with *perspective* since the live room creates that. Even *processing* is applied more as special effect, since rooms will define their own ambience. The other three P's take on some unique perspectives.

Frequency pockets can be an advantage here, too. They help in the studio due to the limitations of speaker reproduction. In the live venue, it's due to the cluttering nature of room acoustics. You will also find your equalizing based on the combination of live and electronic sound. If the sound of the instrument amps and stage monitors produce a lot of low and low mid in the room, you will be more conservative in this area through the main system.

Priorities need to be maintained, and are often in competition with stage levels. Use creative ideas to limit these levels in smaller venues. When instrument amps are mic'ed, coax the performers to face them across stage or back at themselves like stage monitors, and run their volumes at the lowest acceptable levels. Use plexiglass baffles at least 5 feet high around drums as necessary, and place some freestanding sound-absorbing baffles in a V shape behind the drums to keep more sound from bouncing off hard back walls. Use your ear, or analyzer, to determine which lower frequencies from the stage monitors are most pronounced in the room and drop these another 3-6dB on the monitor graphic. Most of the time, I choose to EQ everything below 100Hz out of the monitors. This reduces excessive bass buildup on stage and in the room, and gives the monitor system more headroom. All this can greatly improve your control of the mix out front.

Panning[15] brings up another aspect of live sound — whether you should run a monaural or stereo system. Mono is more typical, though it's often just as economical to run stereo with a few advantages. The house signal is divided between two output busses (Left & Right), increasing overall headroom through the system, and some stereo sources such as keyboards, digital effects, or soundtracks have a richer, cleaner sound when their imaging is maintained. You just don't want to be panning mono sources so that the audience sitting on the left side misses stuff you panned towards the right. Remember that most of the audience will not be sitting in the sweet spot where both sides will sound equally balanced.

Systems usually run mono when the operator needs to *group*[16] the channels. On 4- or 8-group consoles, the pans are used in conjunction with the assign switches to feed multiple channels out a common group fader for easy *submaster* control. Then the groups are fed to the main outs. The problem is that all the channels sent to a group are routed through a single fader, hence the group becomes mono. For something like stereo keyboard, you would have to assign to two groups panned in stereo which uses up available groups twice as fast. A way around this is to route stereo stuff directly to the main stereo outs. All the other mono stuff can be grouped as needed.

As I mentioned in the mixer sections, VCAs, DCAs, or digital fader groups offer the best of both worlds. Since their channel groups are created by either linking the motorized faders of the channels or assigning them to dedicated faders which serve as remote controls for channel levels, no mono routing is necessary. Each channel is free to pan, allowing you to group *and* maintain full stereo flexibility.

I use panning for some other live purposes as well, which I'll touch on under Church Sound in this chapter.

Monitors: A smooth sound with emphasis in the 500Hz to 5kHz range and good definition at 2-3kHz is important to clarity that can cut through stage levels. Don't try to blast everything; the sound will just get loud and cluttered and nobody will be happy. Compromise with the performers on balancing the most crucial parts that need to be heard. If levels start getting out of hand or close to feedback, start backing out the less important stuff to accentuate the priorities and clean up the sound. Roll out low end on the monitor EQs to reduce muddiness. (There will generally be plenty of low-end support from the main system.) Small monitors like Galaxy Hot Spots can also help minimize sound bleed and stage level, while multichannel and wireless in-ear monitor systems can eliminate it all together.

Feedback[4]: The best defense is a well-tuned system, hypercardioid mics, and staying within the capabilities of your system and environment. If a consistent feedback area occurs in mains or monitors, locate the one or two sliders on the appropriate graphic EQ that affect it most and *only* lower those slightly. There are typically only two or three spots that need control. Beyond that, you will find yourself progressively dropping *all* your sliders in a snowball effect, losing gain and quality. (More feedback stuff on page 84.) You might consider purchasing a realtime analyzer to help find feedback points or, as a last resort for monitors, a feedback suppressor like a Sabine FBX or DBX Pro AFS unit which is designed to automatically find and remove them.

CHURCH SOUND

The church audio environment is almost a contradiction, just like *sound engineer*. (That's *sound* as in "sane, rational, responsible, wise, perceptive, logical, sober!" I rest my case.) That's because church audio incorporates public speaking, music production, concerts, theatrical presentations, *and* recording. And who typically runs it all? Volunteers!

On top of that, we have a very discerning and broad audience of 1 to 100 year olds who aren't concerned with technicalities. They just want things to sound good and look nice. I can't think of a more complex situation to be in unless you're a pastor who *has* a poor sound system. Then prayer is the first step. This section is the second.

Sanctuary Studios: I use this term because church audio is more of a controlled environment. Once things are set up properly in your room, procedure and operation can be pretty consistent from week to week with few changes except for special presentations. Major emphasis should be on logical system design for ease of use, equipment and settings labeled and logged (or stored on digital equipment) as a constant reference, and one person dedicated to responsibility for operations and related decisions. Too many cooks spoil the broth.

In addition, a well-tuned speaker system will give you an accurate reference, as do studio monitors, allowing you to make proper EQ and balance decisions that transfer favorably to any recording or broadcast applications you may employ.

Speakers: Speaker choices and arrangements are of prime importance. I've seen cheap *and* expensive setups that sounded terrible and only covered half the sanctuary. Obviously, the salesmen or installers didn't have a clue or didn't care. (They may have claimed to be non-denominational, but I'll bet they favored $10's and $20's.)

Line (vertical) arrays offer the most defined and adjustable patterns, coverage, and projection for larger venues, but I would leave these more complex systems to professional installers. For conventional (side-by-side) center arrays, I suggest 2-way speakers with a horizontal horn **dispersion**[23] of 60° to 75° since these will throw more evenly over distance than a 90°. (*No piezo horns!* Refer to the speaker section for more guidance.) Horns should be directed towards the rear seating of the sanctuary with the lower, forward edge of the horn pattern catching the first row.

Speakers with 12" woofers (or smaller) offer better vocal clarity than 15" along with lighter weight, less mass, and lower cost. Any speakers suspended in a center "free field" will lack sub-bass anyway, so add a subwoofer somewhere on the floor or under the staging if strong bass is preferred. If it's a smaller room (no more than 60 feet wide) and speakers are mounted on each side or placed in side chambers, 15" 2-ways without subs can be sufficient due to increased bass efficiency from walls or boundaries. When side placement is appropriate, chambers can also offer a broader sound for music and choir, easier access for maintenance, and a less conspicuous location.

Another consideration is how *sound energy* is concentrated or distributed. If you have center speakers hanging only 10–12 feet over a pulpit due to a low ceiling, all the sound energy will be concentrated directly over some of the more feedback-prone mics, namely the pastor's wireless and the podium mic. Side placement may then be best, splitting the speakers to each side so the sound energy is distributed over a wider field, reducing the feedback potential at any particular spot on stage. Even if the pastor is standing on the far-side floor in front of a speaker, he is only close to half the energy. Also, with smaller rooms, you don't have to be overly concerned with point-source reference since the ambient voice itself can provide that. The speakers merely offer supplemental level and definition.

Determining the best position for speakers takes a lot of consideration. Though a center array can be a safe bet in most rooms, I find multi-point configurations better or even necessary in many average-size facilities due to a trend towards wider or arena-style rooms and stronger music programs. Where I used to believe that a center arrangement was the only appropriate choice (as many sound consultants still do), I eventually discovered that there were more creative approaches to system design beyond the norm. One such approach is what I call **acoustic emulation**. In other words, if individual instruments and vocals can *acoustically* exhibit location and timing differences in a 3-dimensional field, why can't speakers serve to emulate that? With this in mind...

Cluster, LCR, & CS: While road engineers envision line arrays or stacks of speakers on each side, a **central cluster** is the popular arrangement in fixed installations such as sanctuaries or theatre. Though it doesn't have the broad imaging and stereo capability of side placement, it does minimize the phase cancellations caused by timing differences from separated speakers. It also provides a central **point-source reference**, meaning sound is emanating from the direction of the primary action, namely vocals center stage.

Combining a central cluster with side speakers will create a multi-point system. When such a setup is configured to provide the same signal to all speakers for extended coverage of a very wide or odd-shaped room, that's a **center cluster with side fills**. When it is designed to send discreet signals to left, center, and right speakers via the mixer channel pans, that's an **LCR** system. Some major manufacturers make mixing consoles designed for true LCR, but a "pseudo" LCR setup can be accomplished with almost any stereo mixer. One way is to use the stereo out for L-R and a group or matrix output for center. An easier way is to forget about running stereo, which isn't necessary in most live applications, and run the Left output to Center and the Right output to Left-Right speakers in mono. With this **CS** (**C**enter-**S**ides) setup, the channel pan control determines whether a source comes through the center (L), sides (R), or anywhere in between.

The initial idea with LCR was to maintain more accurate direction of live stereo sound consistent with performers' positions on stage, but I contend a more substantial application is to promote better separation between the vocals and the instruments. I often install the dual-mono CS setup in churches and theatre with the center cluster speakers dedicated to vocals, and the side speakers (positioned a little farther back than the center cluster for front-to-back perspective) dedicated to instruments and soundtracks. The quality of sound is significantly improved since vocals and instruments aren't competing with each other through the same speakers in the same dimensional plane. This makes for a clarifying imaging difference which emulates natural acoustics recognizable to our ears: a musical group behind and surrounding the front and center vocalists. This is my usual setup for *acoustic emulation.*

With a CS setup, for example, I can pan the actors, pastors, and lead vocalists full left to the center cluster. Most stage instruments can pan full right to the sides. I would pan soundtracks slightly to the left to fill in a center gap since they don't have any ambient direction from the stage like instruments. (If it's a split track, I can conveniently pan the vocal channel to the cluster and music channel to the sides.) If the primary instrument is piano or acoustic guitar, I can pan that towards the left where it's more out front. Background vocals can be panned slightly to the right to make them a little wider and move them behind the lead, and choir channels can have their pans centered so they come equally through cluster and sides making them broad and deep (like a choir should be). This gives you some idea of the creative and dimensional potential of a CS system.

I usually use 15" 2-way speakers for the music and 12" or smaller on vocals for better definition. If you have subs for L-R, you could opt for 12" full range there, too. (You don't need subs for the vocal cluster.) I've used some powerful 8" waveguides by WorxAudio that worked great for center when small size was an issue for a low ceiling, or when video projection had a tight shot underneath to a screen. As a final note, it's important that the center cluster and side speakers in a CS system each be positioned to perform as full-coverage systems since they are doing individual jobs.

(Note: Always make sure elevated speakers are properly suspended and equipped with safety-approved stand mount or hanging hardware.)

Though I encourage you to consult with a professional on speaker system design, I can offer a few of my personal guidelines:

- *Side Mounting* - rooms with lower ceilings and no more than 60 feet wide with center aisle (minimizes audible phase cancellation). Speakers should be 10–15 feet high, and at least 10 feet back from the first row of seats. Will also cover most balconies.
- *Cluster* - rooms with ceilings 20 feet or higher, more than 60 feet wide, or those without center aisle or side placement locations. Centered over pulpit, use two speakers arrayed to cover 100° to 120°, 3 or 4 for arc seating requiring wider coverage. Horns should be at least 15–20 feet high depending on depth of room and possible balcony coverage.
- *Multi Point* - a combination of the previous two, either as CS or side fill, for larger rooms or those wider than they are deep. (Can also be used when lower ceilings demand that sound be supplemented through side speakers to distribute sound energy.)

Rooms seating over 1,000 or those with unusual acoustics (I once evaluated a sanctuary that had so many reflections arriving simultaneously at one spot, it created its own pitch!), or complex balcony or side-wing construction will require more strategic design. Some will require line array or a combination of cluster, side fills, and delayed-speaker arrangements. Leave it to the professionals unless you're real brave and the church is very forgiving.

Stereo Tracks: Churches often use stereo cassette or CD soundtracks for singers and choirs. Unfortunately with cassette, mono sound systems can cause some high-frequency phase cancellation between the left and right tracks. This is the result of the tape not aligning perfectly on the deck's heads. Stereo operation eliminates any audible problem. If you're not running stereo, use only one side of the cassette output (preferably the left to accommodate the music side of "split tracks"), or run the channel of the right side lower than the other to minimize phasing effects. Thankfully, cassette soundtracks are on the way out due to the better quality, durability, and cueing of CDs. CDs don't have the phasing problem since they are read digitally, not mechanically.

You can develop some "conducting" capabilities for music tracks as if you were leading an orchestra. Make sure soft beginnings are raised enough for the singers to get their cues. If dynamics seem to be lacking, you can drop back music slightly during verses and gradually swell the music while the last note is being held. You'd be surprised at the extra impact such subtle changes will add to a performance and an otherwise "flat" background. If necessary, consult with your music director on these techniques.

Feedback Control[4]: Choir and lapel mics cause some of the greatest feedback difficulties, and they're good reason to insist on a mixer with at least one sweep frequency in the channel EQ. Without it, you can't address specific problem areas for individual mics. First step is finding and controlling the few major feedback points, thereby smoothing out most of the rough spots. Afterwards, you just have to be mindful that you have some limit to any given mic's level before feedback will start. Assuming you have at least 3-band, sweep mid EQ . . .

Gradually bring up a problem channel until slight, controlled feedback starts. If the feedback tone is a very low or very high frequency, cut back the appropriate fixed EQ knob a notch or two. If the tone sounds more in the vocal range, turn the mid-frequency knob all the way to the right, set the mid-gain control at 10:00, then rotate the frequency knob to the left until you hear the feedback dip or stop. Set the sweep at that point, then bring up the fader more to find and work out the next feedback point. If it's a previous one again, drop the appropriate EQ gain another notch. If it's a mid problem close to the first, you may be able to compromise the sweep frequency position along with a notch less mid gain to catch them both. Try for a third feedback frequency unless you start getting two or three at once. Then stop. To go further will likely get you to the point of diminishing returns. Finish up by making subtle EQ adjustments for voice quality if necessary.

With a well-tuned system, I almost always have to roll back somewhere between 400Hz to 800Hz, as well as some low end on choir mics and omni lapels. (For the latter, try between 500Hz and 630Hz first.) The miniature podium condensers may require some similar adjustments. Good handheld mics don't give me any trouble, but acoustic piano mics may, depending on the level needed from them. Watch your stage-monitor levels, too. If there is a consistent problem frequency here, take it down slightly on the monitor graphic EQ. If you have trouble locating feedback, consider purchasing a **realtime analyzer** (p. 52, SIGNAL CORPS, Realtime Analyzer). The answers will light up before your very eyes and before long, you'll be able to approximate frequencies by ear.

I have a method for setting level on the most finicky mics to make it easy for the sound team to avoid feedback during the service — from the system *and* the pastor. After equalizing a lapel or podium mic, I'll bring down the input gain, set the channel fader at the *unity gain* "0" position, bring up the input gain until feedback starts, then back off a notch or so. I'll also set choir mics this way with *all* their faders up to account for the collective level. Once finished, I know that "0" is the highest I can safely go on the fader(s), and any higher will be shaky ground. (And we all know *shaky ground* and *solid rock* don't mix.)

Phase Reverse[14]: There may come a time when a pastor with an active wireless lapel walks up to an active podium mic, and his voice suddenly becomes very thin or hollow sounding. This is an indication that the mics are out of phase. If you have phase reverse on your mixer, you could switch it on the podium mic. If not, reverse the hot and neutral on one end of the podium mic cable. (You could pursue these solutions for the wireless receiver cable instead if you are using balanced XLR.) Also, due to distance phase effects, it would be best to commit to one mic or the other instead of leaving them both on even when they are wired in phase. Wireless wins if the pastor moves around.

Another phase effect can be caused by sound bouncing into a mic off a hard podium surface. If you notice a problem, try some carpeting on its surface to absorb reflections. (You may be able to get away with light gray or white on a clear plexiglass podium. Clear carpet is very expensive and hard to come by.)

Right-Wing Engineering: The catchword for conservative engineering in smaller rooms is sound *reinforcement*, not *replacement*. Think about how close you can stay to natural sound levels rather than how much you can overpower them. In most churches, you'll be able to hear at least some of the singers and pastor's voice carry acoustically in the room. It just wouldn't be enough to distinguish everything clearly and get over music or background noise. So add just the level needed to accomplish that. Then sound retains a more natural quality. As with micing, trust your ear. If you can't hear what's being said, others won't be able to either. If it's loud to you, it's probably blasting Grandma in the front row. Use common sense for the common good.

A service can include spontaneous activity from pastors, music leaders, or members of the congregation as they are felt led. Don't be a robot, but be aware of what is going on and prepared to bring up speaking or wireless mics as needed. Most pastors have certain moves they make that indicate they're about to speak, so try to second-guess them. Don't wait until after they start before you bring them up, and don't use channel on/off switches for them. Use the faders for more gradual changes in case you miss a cue. In fact, I prefer to leave a pastor's wireless preset and let them cut their transmitter on/off as they choose. This takes the heat off us, but ultimately it's the pastor's choice. They have enough to think about without adapting to our whims.

Concentrate on the main music leader and instrument, normally piano or acoustic guitar, in the monitors. These will provide the primary vocal, pitch, and rhythm reference for all concerned. Be careful about trying to feed choir, lapel, or omni earworn mics through nearby monitors since they're more prone to feedback. And, as I mentioned in chapter 3, if you need more choir level in the mains to get over full band and orchestra, try inconspicuous micing of eight to ten primary choir singers with mini-earworn wireless like the Audio-Technica Microset. A little expense, but it works great!

Another note about vocal mics. Some think that you need to have mics meticulously tuned for each person. This may be practical in professional concerts, but is not necessary in the normal worship environment where you have background vocalists changing every week and/or engineers who may be "unreliable" when it comes to EQ technique. If you have matching mics tuned with equal fidelity and clarity, you will be reproducing each vocal the way it sounds naturally. Unless someone has a really bad vocal tone, why would you want to try to make everyone sound identical? The differences can actually enhance the density and separation of vocal parts as they would if singing without a sound system. The moral: keep it simple, tune all your BGV mics the same, there will be less room for error, and the mics will work for any singers you put on them.

Hearing-Assistance: Like wireless in-ear monitors, hearing-assistance systems by companies like Telex, Williams, Sennheiser and a few others offer more economical wireless transmission for the hard-of-hearing used in churches and other public venues. Since a common signal from the mixer will suffice for all these listeners (I usually use an aux or matrix feed), you can have a single transmitter and any number of wireless receivers on the same frequency to pass out to those who need them. Sometimes a convenience that's easy on church funds is for users to buy their own personal receivers and bring them to services. You can also use receivers in the nursery (if the system will transmit that far) so you won't need a remote speaker system that might wake the babies. Listening options include single and dual earbuds, or induction loops that will transmit the receiver signal into hearing aids.

These systems can also be useful for some alternate purposes if you use your imagination. Most transmitters will accept a mic input as well, so I've used them to transmit foreign language translations to non-English speaking members of a congregation. Simply put the translator on headphones to hear the pastor, give him the mic connected to an HA transmitter, and pass out the receivers. Though most economical HA systems are low band and lack quality for more crucial applications, the Galaxy AnySpot is high-band UHF designed to serve as a wireless IEM as well. This means you can pass a receiver to a choir/orchestra director to serve as in-ear monitor on those occasions when directing a cantata from the floor. (I'd hate to have them tripping on monitor cables right at the climax of Handel's *Messiah*.)

Service Recording: Some mixers provide dedicated outputs for recording, but they are simply paralleled off the main outputs and probably won't give you a worthy mix unless it is sermon alone. Normally, you should use a *post-fader* aux send for easy individual channel control to the recording. If you don't have an aux send available and you're running a basic mono system, a convenient way to get an easy and individual recording feed from a stereo mixer is to use the Left output for live sound and the Right for recording. ("L" and "R." How convenient.) Start with all the channel pans centered. If certain channels are too loud on tape, pan them sufficiently to the left reducing their level through the right output. If you use dedicated mics to record the congregation, pan them full right so they only go to the recording. Once these compensated recording "pan-levels" are set, normal operation for the house will balance properly on the recording. Such recording feeds are also useful for broadcast and hearing-assistance systems as well as peripheral speakers in the foyer, halls, nursery, etc.

One tool that is finally catching on in ministry is CDR recording and duplication. Churches are transitioning to this technology since cost has dropped below that of cassette duplicators, there are less maintenance costs and concerns, CD quality is far superior, blank CDRs are much cheaper than the lowest-grade cassette tape, there are flexible on-CD printing options, and audio can be transferred easily to computer for archiving, editing, and web access.

Though I'm sure we'll see a lot of creative products over time, one unique CDR tool is the Copywriter Live from Microboards, which records and duplicates in a self-contained, 2-drive model. In addition to individual recording and high duplication speed, the drives offer a continuous-recording mode by automatically overlapping to the next drive before time runs out. You can also record two separate CDs for Worship and Sermon by simply switching recording drives at appropriate points in the program. This is great if you need to record a complete service that exceeds 80 minutes (the max time for a 700MB CDR), plus your sermons will be archived separately for easy duplication of sermon series. Add an 8-drive tower duplicator, and you can run off high quantities of CDs in house.

(Note: Be aware of laws about duplicating copyrighted music in church programs. Contact licensing organizations like CCLI about restrictions and clearances.)

Following are some final notes:
- Choose a mixer with phantom power and at least one sweep EQ on channels.
- Always buy low-impedance mics. (These use XLR, not 1/4" phone plugs.)
- With cassette recording, use a quick-reverse deck so you don't miss anything.
- For safety, consider mounting a *wireless* mic in the baptismal when needed.
- Don't buy PA speakers with "piezo" horns. For stage monitors, they'll do.
- Always make sure elevated speakers are properly suspended and equipped with safety-approved standmount or hanging hardware.
- Always commend the worship leader on how lovely (he/she) looks today.

THEATRICAL SOUND

Theatre is very similar to church in that natural sound quality is a priority, especially with all the speaking parts involved. Due emphasis should be given to the natural blend of ambient and reinforced sound. A speaker combination of central cluster (for vocals) and mono or stereo side arrangement (for score) can be ideal for musicals with pre-recorded or sequenced tracks, and may not be too difficult given the flexibility of many stage layouts.

I also address this application specifically because of the potential number of wireless employed and the problems of amplifying all the dialog or singing with numerous mics. Unfortunately, the distance and movement of actors onstage often renders fixed-mic pickup ineffective. Sometimes an upstage floor-mounted unidirectional boundary mic like the Crown PCC-160 or a hanging choir mic can work for picking up individuals within an 8' square, or group speaking or singing within 15' if the system is tuned well and the actors can project and e-n-u-n-c-i-a-t-e. Otherwise, wireless lapel or mini-earworn mics are going to be your best bet.

For most situations including churches and schools, $300 to $600 UHF wireless by companies like Audio-Technica, Sennheiser, and Shure do very well. You'll always need to be careful of damage to transmitter parts and cable connections, and you should keep receivers elevated and within 75 feet of the stage if possible to avoid dropouts. Arrange workable mic passes to other actors if you're short a few systems. You could also purchase extra mics which can be precisely placed on performers ahead of time, and just exchange transmitters for quicker mic passes. This is even more economical using the inexpensive EX-503 omni lapel made by Azden, which has a right-angle mini-phone plug for less stress and is compatible with current Sennheiser EW systems. (See more about this and other wireless system tips in the chapter "Unplugged.")

Lapel mics are often worn on the chest, but can also be hidden in the hair or placed over the ear. In the absence of sinus problems, nostril placement offers excellent pickup if you can successfully hide the cable. (Now truthfully, how many of you actually considered this for a second?) I have also been able to spray paint mics and cables with Krylon to match hair, flesh, or clothing colors, but be sure to cover the mic element and plugs while doing so. A great new addition is the "near invisible" mini-earworn mics which come in a few different colors to blend with skin tones or beards. Though considerably higher in cost, they offer much better level and sound quality if you don't mind them being barely visible from the front rows. For stability, you can secure their behind-the-ear cables with clear surgical tape. Make sure the mic follows tight to the cheek line or is hidden in a beard to be as inconspicuous as possible.

With the physical nature of some dramatic productions, be ready for potential problems caused by perspiration getting into mic connections. To remedy this, place the mic in a dry area or seal vulnerable connectors with clear silicone sealer. Another important preventative is to tape over transmitter and mic on/off switches if they don't have a cover or locking feature so they don't accidentally get switched off during a performance. Leave any active indicators visible if possible, and use gaffer's tape (not masking or duct tape) to avoid sticky glue buildup on the transmitter. You may also want to tape down non-locking mic plugs.

When engineering for the theatre, you've got to stay on top of the dialog and make script notations accordingly. I notate mic numbers in the script margins in place of names when mic passes are involved. Circling the number where the actor first enters is a good mic cue, and a "# Off" where they exit makes sure they aren't live offstage. In a particular scene, I'll have all the appropriate mics up to moderate levels and ride them up and down as lines are spoken. Be sure to notate loud passages like yells, screams, whistles, etc. for a quick adjustment to avoid a few migraines in the audience. Digital mixers offer the distinct advantages of compressors on every channel to control levels and memory recall to make sure numerous mics in a particular scene are all up at the touch of a button.

You'll also notice that actors can be picked up through each other's mics if they are close to one another. To minimize the resulting effects, either ride their mics up and down accordingly or commit to one mic if there is good pickup and little movement between the actors. As you become familiar with the parts and dialogue, you can actually get into a rhythm just as the actors do. If there are pre-recorded music and sound effects cues, have someone else control them to keep you free for the wireless. It takes good script notes and some practice, but it's a rewarding feeling when the spontaneous spirit of engineering and dramatic performance come together as one soul-stirring entity.

SO, DO I HAVE TO PAINT YOU A PICTURE?

I guess you thought I'd forget! Yes, I understand how difficult it can be to put the whole thing together without a chart. I, too, have tried putting together Christmas toys! (Take my word for it, audio is easier.) So as a final touch, I've included a graphic diagram of a complete sound system on the next page with the major components, their page locations, and indications of connections and signal flow. A lot of these components will be hidden within digital mixers and processors, but "virtual" connection and operation will follow the same guidelines. Illustrations such as this are provided in many equipment manuals (and should be), so refer to them for more specific information and various applications.

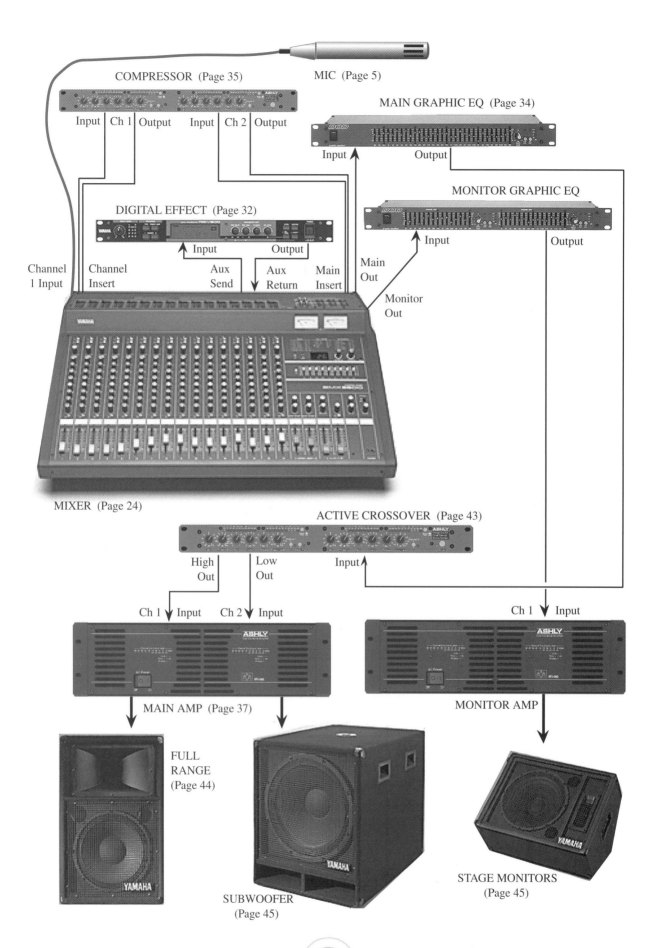

COMPRESSOR (Page 35)

MIC (Page 5)

MAIN GRAPHIC EQ (Page 34)

Input | Ch 1 | Output   Input | Ch 2 | Output

Input   Output

MONITOR GRAPHIC EQ

DIGITAL EFFECT (Page 32)

Input   Output

Input   Output

Channel
1 Input

Channel
Insert

Aux
Send

Aux
Return

Main
Insert

Main
Out

Monitor
Out

MIXER (Page 24)

ACTIVE CROSSOVER (Page 43)

High
Out

Low
Out

Input

Ch 1 | Input   Ch 2 | Input

Ch 1 | Input

MAIN AMP (Page 37)

MONITOR AMP

FULL
RANGE
(Page 44)

STAGE MONITORS
(Page 45)

SUBWOOFER
(Page 45)

14. PACKING UP

Well, I think I've covered about everything I wanted to and, quite frankly, I've run out of vocabulary. I pretty much stuck to what was in my head (as opposed to other areas), and I can't begin to remember where it all came from. A lot of trial and error, and a few major screwups for sure. And it surprised me almost as much as my wife that this much stuff was actually in my head! (Then she wonders why I can't remember to take out the trash. Data banks full, I explain.)

There are lots of good books that specialize in various areas of audio, and I encourage you to pursue them as your desire dictates. I hope I've provided you with an abundance of valuable information here. If not, I probably won't retire with lots of book revenues, so I'll settle for my guitar and some Arby's coupons. Good luck to you, too. I trust you'll enjoy the same satisfaction and rewards that I have in this exciting, challenging, and ever-changing world of pro audio. Take your time, and thank you for giving me some of it.

"There's no business like show business, like no business I know . . ."

P.S. I wouldn't want to disappoint those of you who thought this section was about packing up equipment: *"Don't scratch anything, and put the heavy stuff up front."*

For those of you who may wish to contact me with questions, comments, or critique (be gentle)...

Email: iwhite@sanctuarysound.com

Snailmail: Ira White c/o Sanctuary Sound
5660 E. Virginia Beach Blvd.
Norfolk, VA 23502

INDEX

ABOUT THE AUTHOR

Ira White has been involved in the music business since 1971. Born in Norfolk, Virginia, he began playing professionally as a guitarist/singer in various touring bands. He put together his first 8-track personal studio in 1983, which eventually expanded into a 16-track commercial production facility. Work in retail music sales as well as live recording and sound engineering in concert, theatre, and church venues were a progressive outgrowth of his interests and contacts.

In 1992, he started Studio Street in Virginia Beach, a pro audio store and consulting/install firm which evolved into Sanctuary Sound, Inc. He also works as sound director for a local church, serves as a worship leader, and is involved in independent recording and engineering. Ira released his Christian praise CD in 2004 entitled *Road to Holiness*, and other recent sound projects have included *TMCJ International* theatrical productions and the *Lion of Judah* tour for worship artist Paul Wilbur.

Ira resides in Portsmouth, VA with his wife Susan. His hobbies are scuba diving, traveling, and discussing audio with his dog Mercy who has excellent high-frequency perception. Ira's music website can be found at *www.audiostreet.net/irawhite*.

MORE BOOKS FROM

◢ HAL•LEONARD®

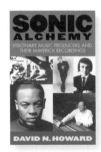

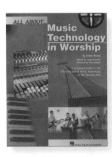

HOME STUDIO CLINIC
A MUSICIAN'S GUIDE TO PROFESSIONAL RECORDING
by Emile Menasché

Written from a musician's point of view, this book is designed to help you build and use a studio based on your musical goals. By exploring concepts and various common tasks, this reader-friendly book gives you the know-how to choose equipment that suits your needs and style, and the techniques to use it effectively.

_____00331466...\$24.95
(ISBN 1-4234-1807-7) (UPC 8-84088-10349-1)

THE ULTIMATE LIVE SOUND OPERATOR'S HANDBOOK
by Bill Gibson

High-quality audio is imperative, whether you're running sound for a rock, country, punk, or jazz band performing in clubs, arenas, or outdoor parks. This comprehensive handbook focuses on each aspect of live sound in a way that is easy to understand, breaking the process down into principles and practices that assist the modern sound tech in everything from planning and budgeting to mixing and recording the live show.

_____00331469...\$34.95
(ISBN 1-4234-1971-5) (UPC 8-84088-10676-8)

101 RECORDING TIPS
STUFF ALL THE PROS KNOW AND USE
by Adam St. James
Book/CD Pack

Tips, suggestions, advice, and other useful information garnered through a lifetime of home and pro studio recording adventures. It's an essential collection of tricks of the trade that will improve anyone's home or pro studio recordings. The accompanying CD includes nearly one hour of audio demonstrations.

_____00311035...\$14.95
(ISBN 0-634-06562-9) (UPC 0-73999-86774-9)

ALL ABOUT HARD DISK RECORDERS
AN INTRODUCTION TO THE CREATIVE WORLD OF DIGITAL, HARD DISK RECORDING
by Robby Berman

This book takes you from the very beginning with an overview, to practical tips for taking advantage of the choices you have with this flexible recording system. Topics include: setting up a hard drive; principles of audio editing; maintaining a hard drive; how a work station operates; and more.

_____00331033...\$19.95
(ISBN 0-634-05734-0) (UPC 0-73999-60832-8)

ALL ABOUT MUSIC TECHNOLOGY IN WORSHIP
HOW TO SET UP AND PLAN A MUSICAL PERFORMANCE
by Steve Young
edited by Corey Fournier

Church musicians today must possess a working knowledge of music technology to offer their music ministry in the varied and demanding settings of worship. This book provides simple instructions on everything from synthesizers, MIDI, and sequencing to percussion, bass, and guitar technology.

_____00331034...\$19.95
(ISBN 0-634-05449-X) (UPC 0-73999-54088-8)

THE BASICS OF LIVE SOUND
TIPS, TECHNIQUES & LUCKY GUESSES
by Jerry J. Slone

This beginner's guide provides easy-to-understand coverage aimed at the novice on topics such as: sound and hearing; microphone models, specs, and techniques; mixers; equalization; amplifiers; speakers; the audio chain; schools and universities for continuing education; and more.

_____00330779...\$9.95
(ISBN 0-634-03028-0) (UPC 0-73999-30779-5)

THE DESKTOP STUDIO
by Emile Menasché

With the right software, your computer can be a recorder, mixer, editor, video production system, and even a musical instrument. *The Desktop Studio* will help you get the most out of your computer and turn it – and you – into a creative powerhouse. It is a fully illustrated, comprehensive look at software and hardware, and provides expert tips for getting the most out of your music computer.

_____00330783...\$22.95
(ISBN 0-634-03019-1) (UPC 0-73999-65680-0)

LIVE SOUND FOR MUSICIANS
by Rudy Trubitt

Live Sound for Musicians shows you how to keep your band's PA system working smoothly, from set-up and soundcheck right through your performance. If you're the person in the band who runs the PA, this is the book you've been waiting for!

_____00330249...\$19.95
(ISBN 0-7935-6852-8) (UPC 0-73999-79303-1)

SONIC ALCHEMY
VISIONARY MUSIC PRODUCERS AND THEIR MAVERICK RECORDINGS
by David N. Howard

You may not have heard of them, but you have certainly heard their songs! From the lo-fidelity origins of early pioneers to today's dazzling technocrats, this book explores the influence of these visionary music producers through popular music and the crucial role they have played in shaping the way we hear music today.

_____00331051...\$18.95
(ISBN 0-634-05560-7) (UPC 0-73999-77098-8)

CHURCH SOUND SYSTEMS
by Lonnie Park

This easy-to-understand book is for everyone involved with church sound. Whether you want to design a new system or get the most out of the one you have, this handy guide will help you let your message be heard! It covers everything you need to know about: design and layout of your sound system; choosing the right microphones; speaker setup and positioning; mixers; and much more.

_____00330542...\$12.95
(ISBN 0-634-01782-9) (UPC 0-73999-23923-2)

FOR MORE INFORMATION, SEE YOUR LOCAL MUSIC DEALER, OR WRITE TO:

◢ HAL•LEONARD®
CORPORATION
7777 W. BLUEMOUND RD. P.O. BOX 13819 MILWAUKEE, WI 53213